Name ______________________________

Practice 1.1

P9-DER-504

Top, Middle, Bottom

1

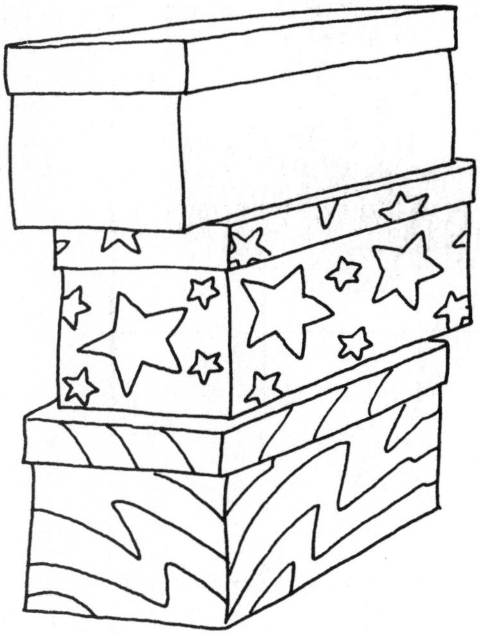

2

3

4

Directions: 1–4 Color the item in the middle green, the item on top red, and the item on the bottom yellow.

Use with Teacher's Edition pages 5A–6.

Name ____________________

Before, After, Between

1

2

3

4

Directions: **1** Circle the rabbit that is before the animal in a cap. **2** Circle the animal that is after the one in a cap. **3** Circle the animal that is before the one in a cap. **4** Circle the animal that is between the ones in caps.

Use with Teacher's Edition pages 7A–8.

Name ______________________________

Inside, Outside

1

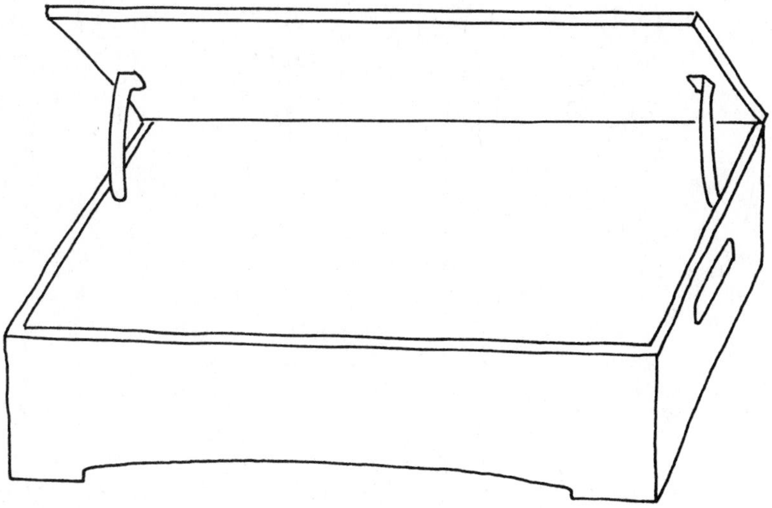

2

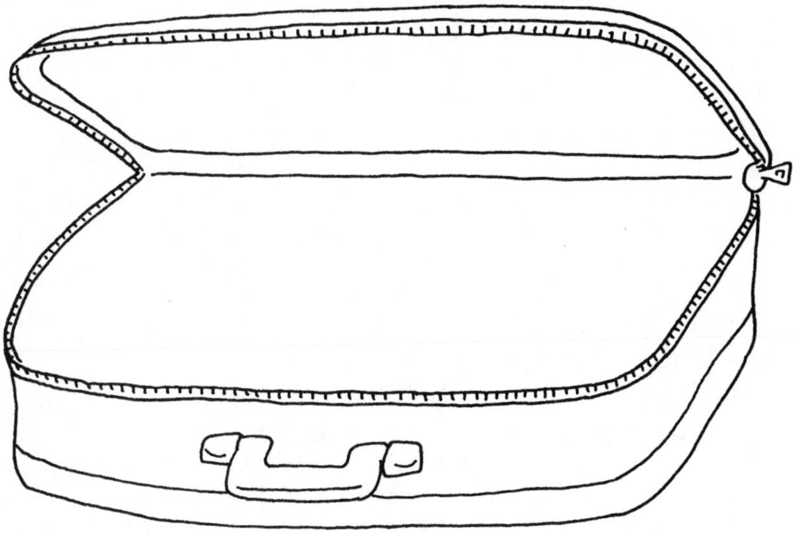

Directions: **1** Draw something blue inside the toy box. Draw something orange outside the toy box. **2** Draw something green inside the suitcase. Draw something red outside the suitcase.

Use with Teacher's Edition pages 9A–10.

Name ______________________________

Practice 1.4

Left and Right

1

2

3

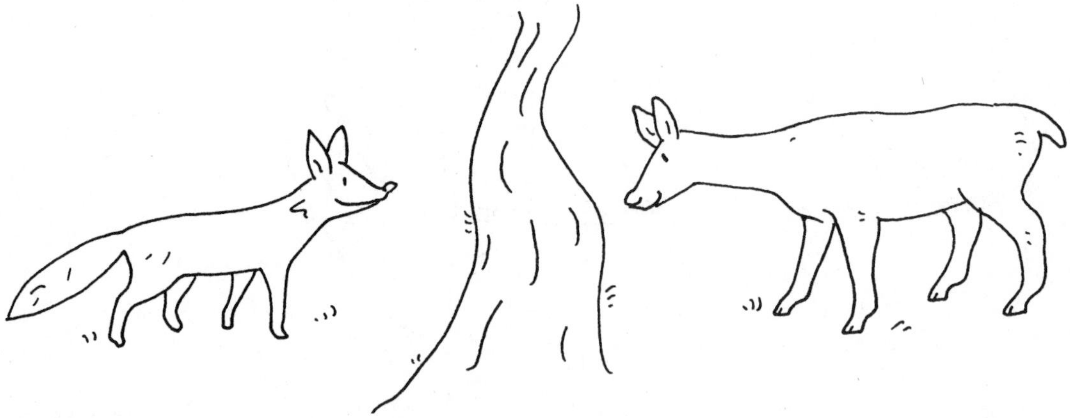

Directions: **1** Color the dog on the left blue and the one on the right red. **2** Color the tree on the left green and the one on the right yellow. **3** Color the animal on the left orange and the one on the right brown.

Use with Teacher's Edition pages 10A–10D.

Name ______________________________

More Position Words

Directions: Color blue the child on top of the slide. Color green the child coming down. Color yellow a child walking over something. Color red a child going up. Color orange a child crawling under something.

Use with Teacher's Edition pages 10E–10H.

Name ______________________________

Practice 1.6

Patterns With Sounds and Motions

1

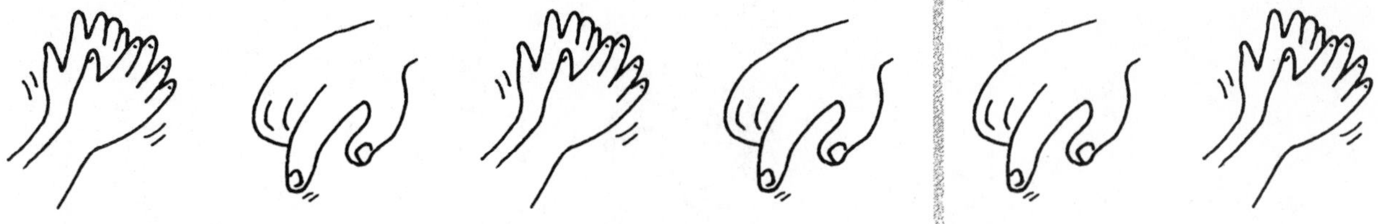

2

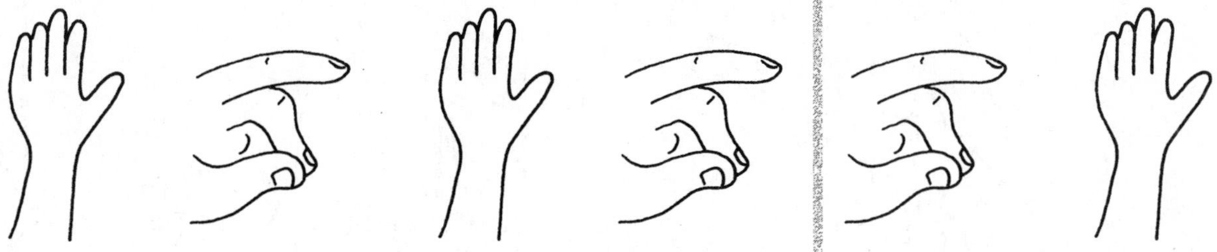

3

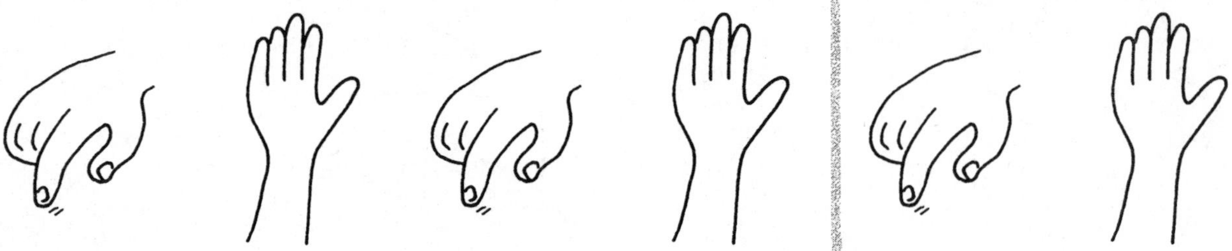

4

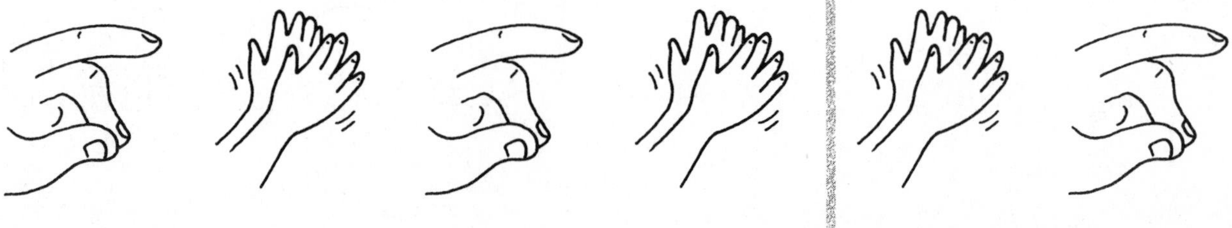

Directions: 1–4 Look at the pattern. Circle the picture that shows what action comes next.

Use with Teacher's Edition pages 10I–10L.

Name ______________________________

Practice 1.7

Extend Patterns

1

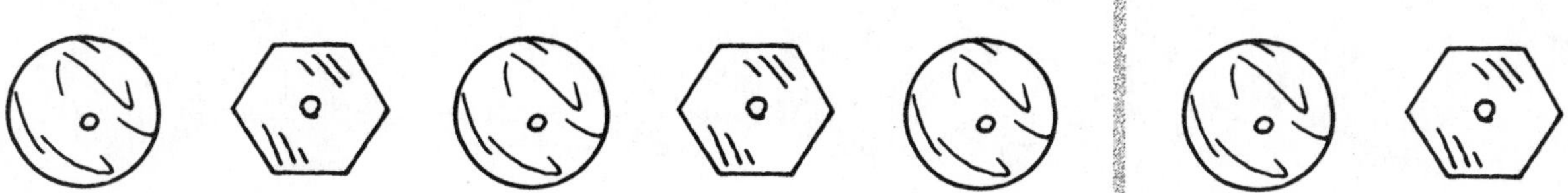

2

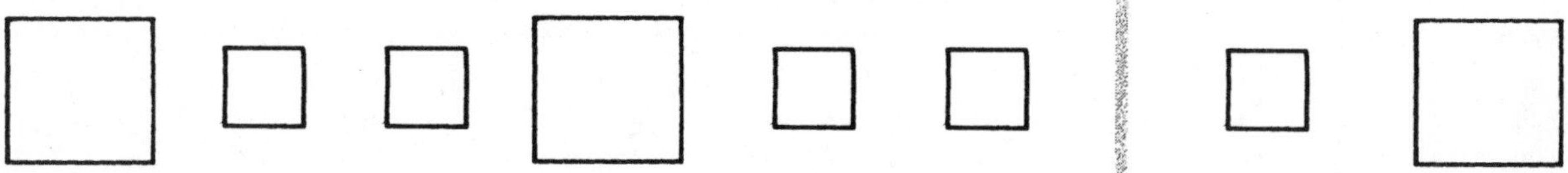

3

4

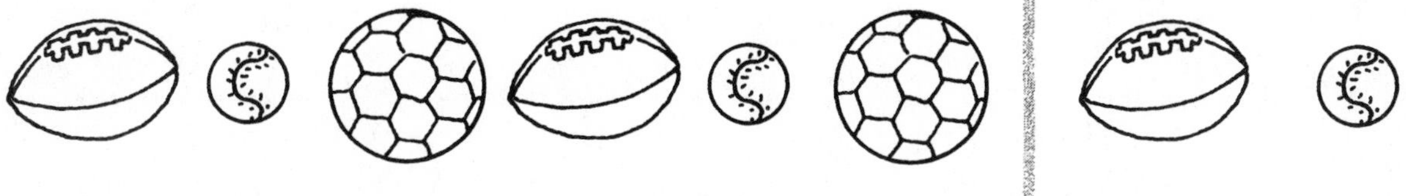

5

Directions: **1–5** Look at the pattern. Circle the item that is likely to come next in the pattern.

Use with Teacher's Edition pages 11A–12.

Name ______________________________

Make Patterns

1

2

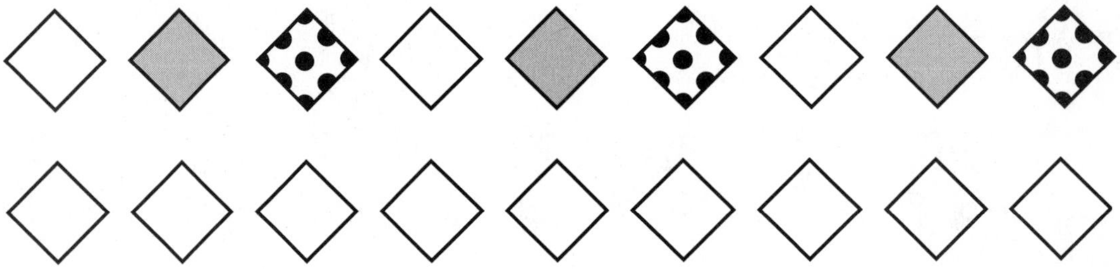

3

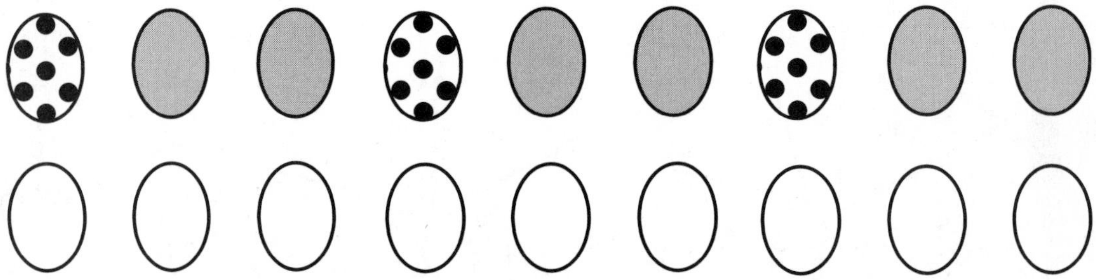

Directions: **1–3** Find the pattern. Show the same pattern using different colors.

Use with Teacher's Edition pages 13A–14.

Name ______________________________

Problem Solving: Draw a Pattern

1

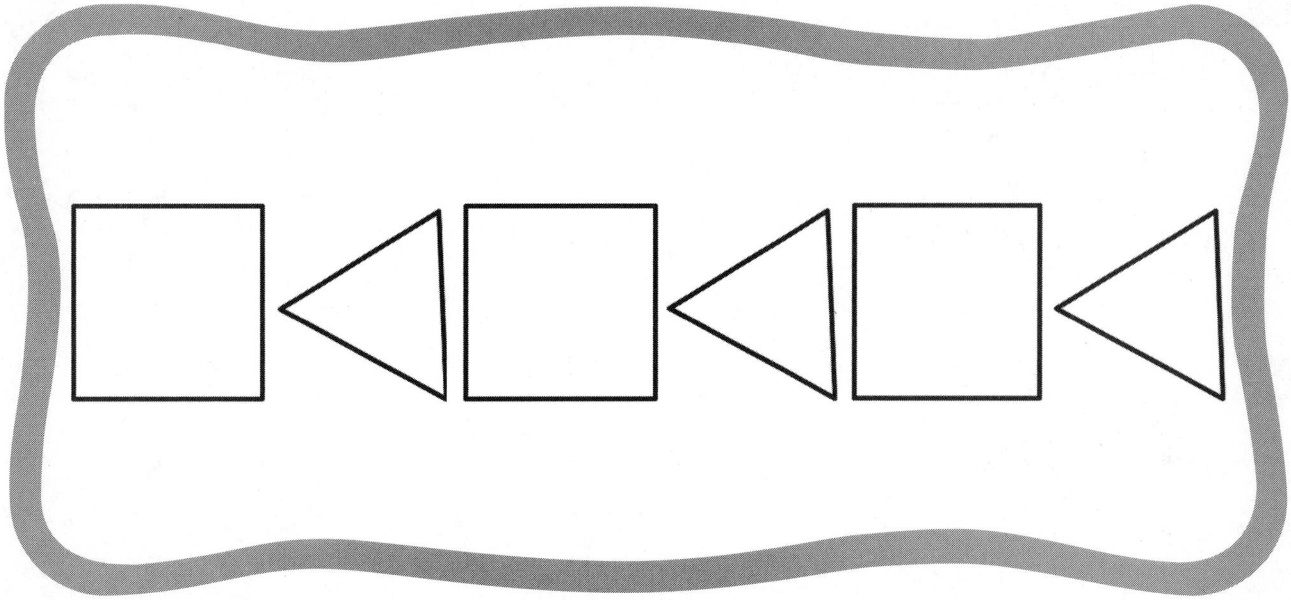

2

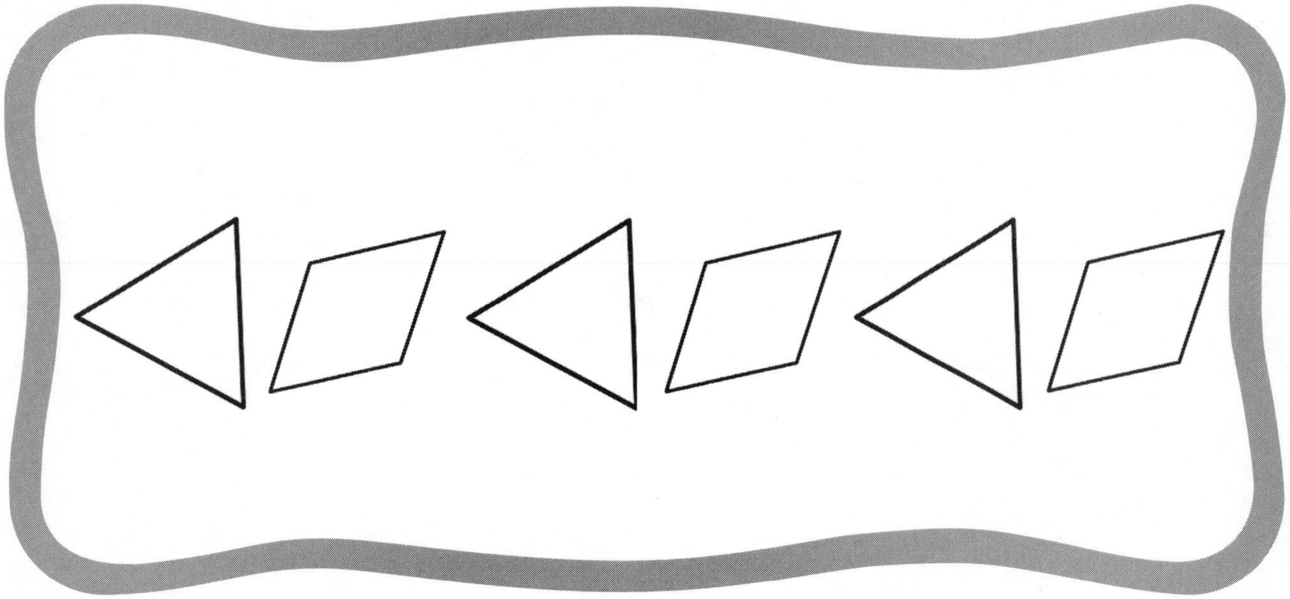

Directions: 1–2 Look at the pattern. Use two different colors to fill in the pattern.

Use with Teacher's Edition pages 15A–16.

Name ______________________________

Practice 2.1

Alike and Different

1

2

3

4

Directions: 1–4 Circle the flowers that are alike. Cross out the one that is different.

Use with Teacher's Edition pages 21A–22.

Name ______________________________

Practice 2.2

Sort by Color

1

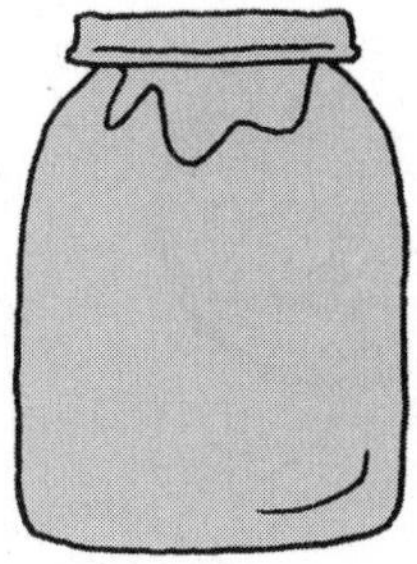

2

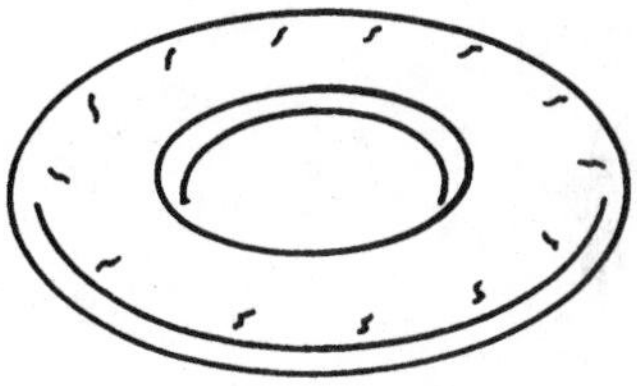

3

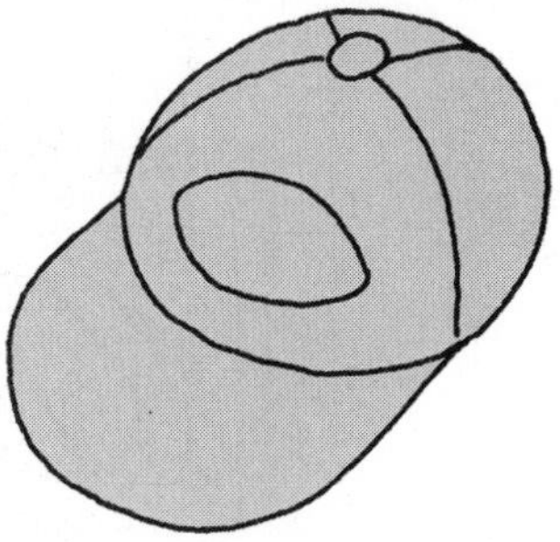

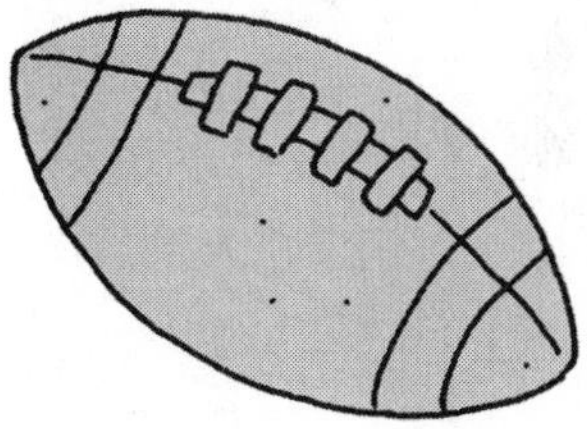

4

Directions: 1–4 Circle the pictures that are the same color.

Use with Teacher's Edition pages 23A–24.

Name ______________________________

Practice 2.3

Sort by Size

1

2

Directions: **1** Color the big coins red. **2** Color the small stamps blue.

Use with Teacher's Edition pages 25A–26.

Name ______________________________

Sort by Shape

1

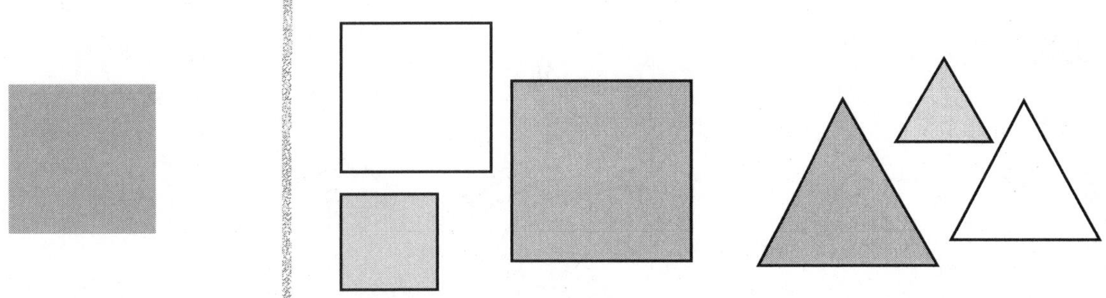

2

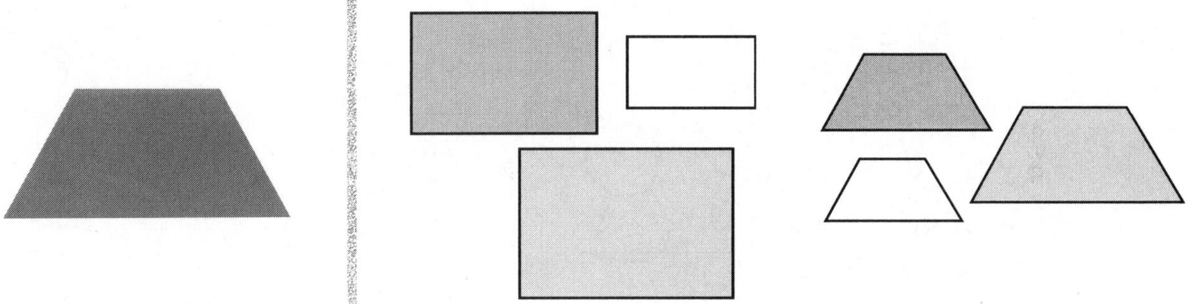

3

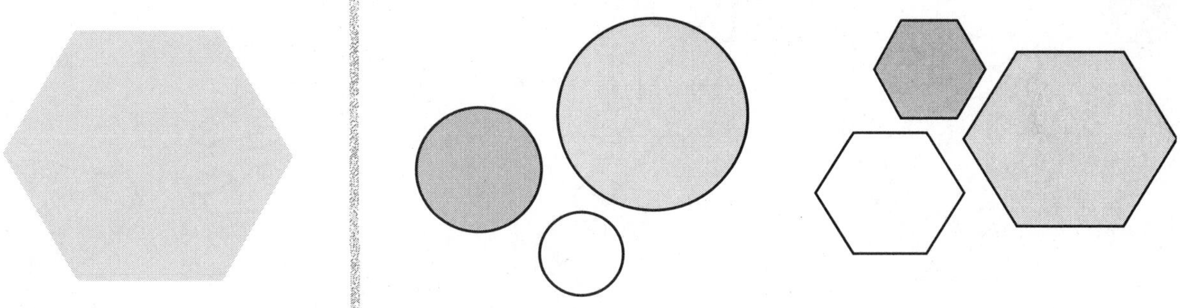

4

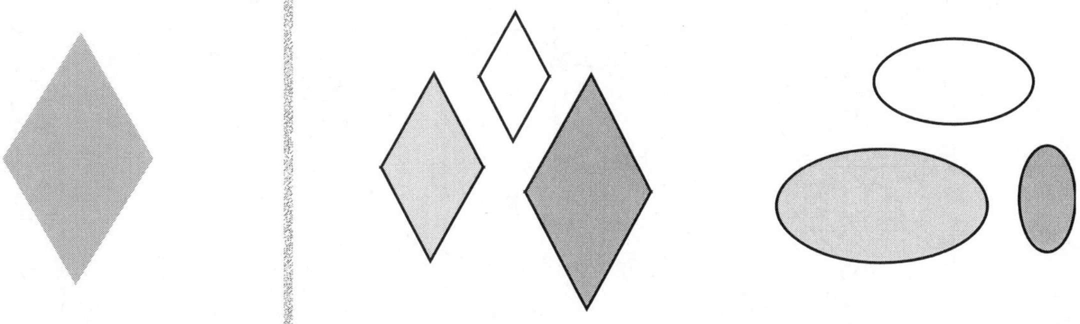

Directions: 1–4 Circle the group where the shape belongs.

Use with Teacher's Edition pages 27A–28.

Name ____________________

Sort by Kind

1

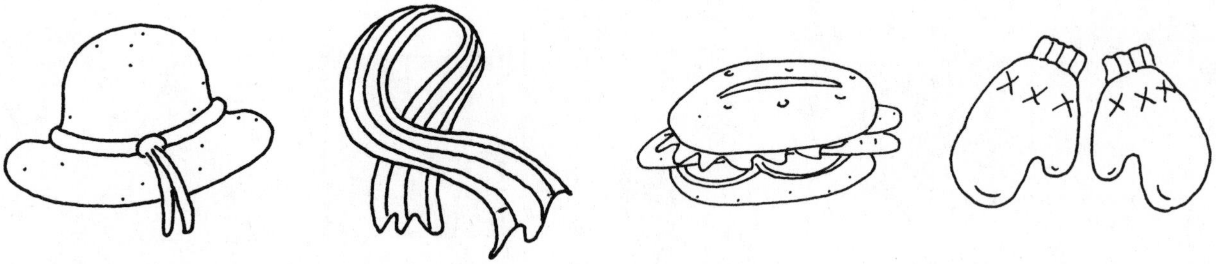

2

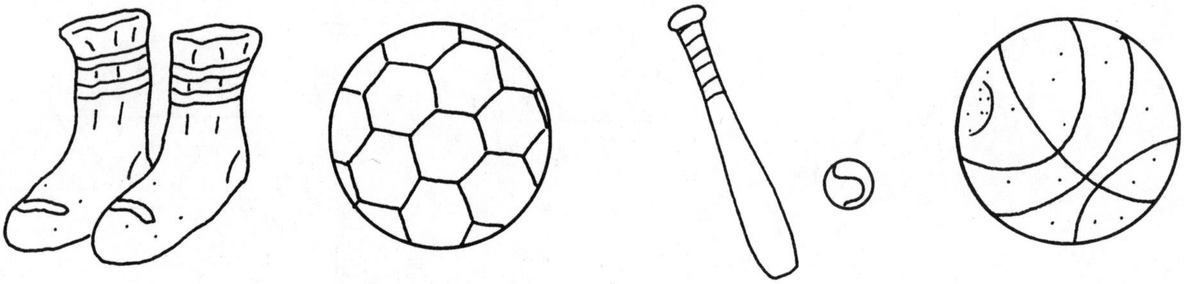

3

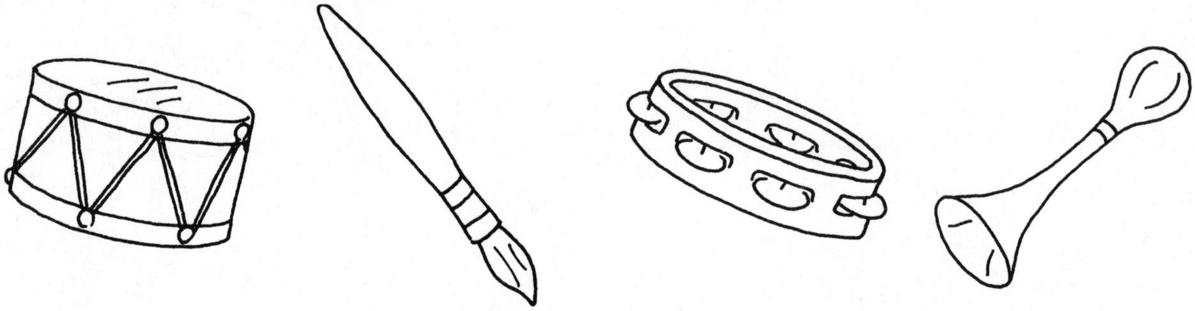

4

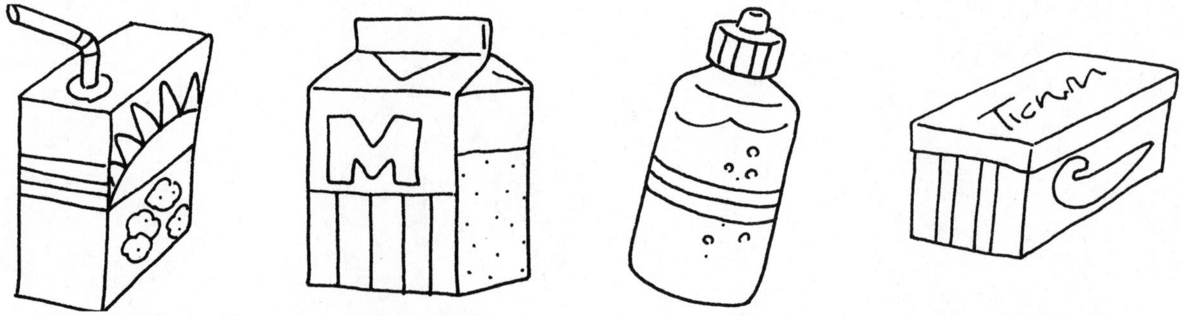

Directions: Circle the items that show: **1** things you wear, **2** games you can play, **3** things that make music, and **4** things you drink.

Use with Teacher's Edition pages 29A–30.

Name ____________________

Sort by Own Rule

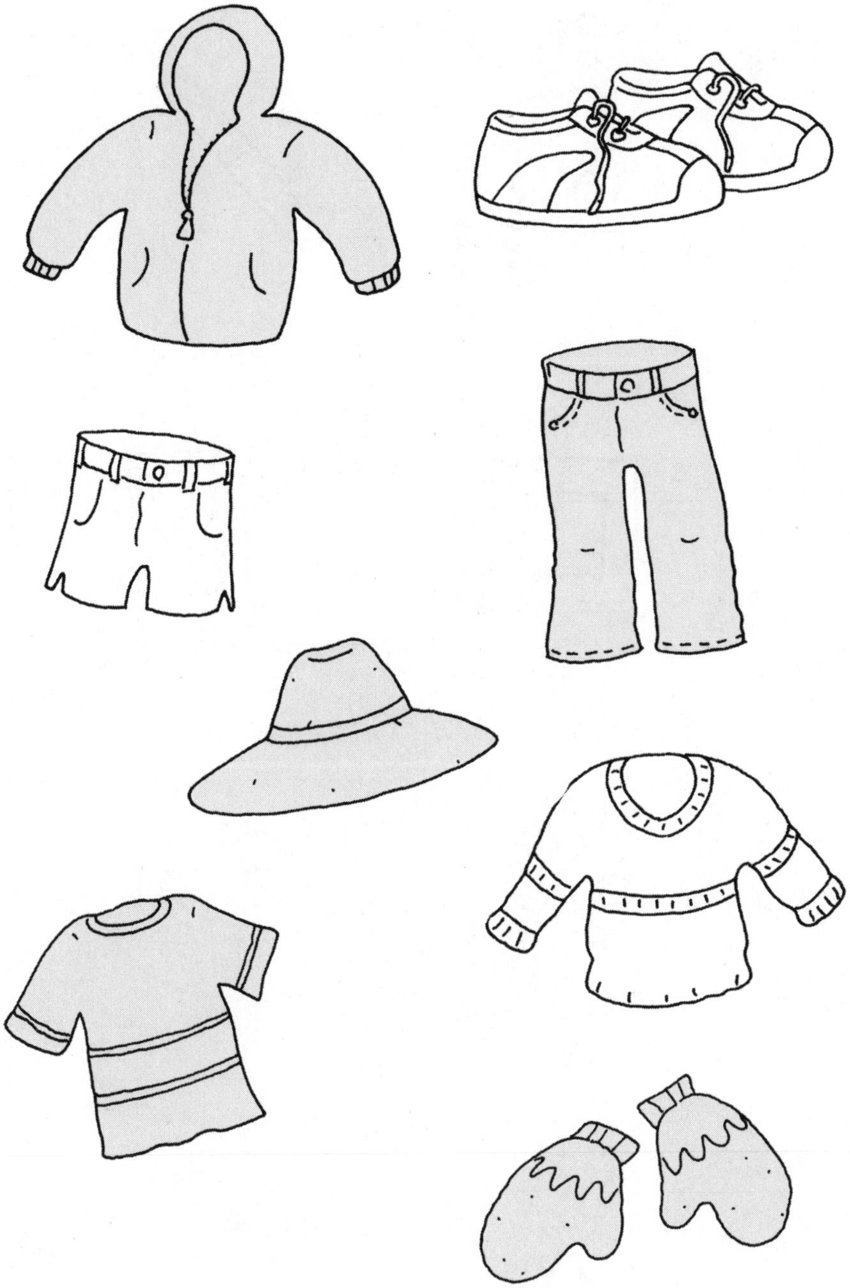

Directions: Think of a sorting rule. Color blue the things you would put in one group. Color green the things you would put in the other group. Tell about your sorting rule.

Use with Teacher's Edition pages 31A–32.

Name ______________________________

Problem Solving: Use Logical Reasoning

1

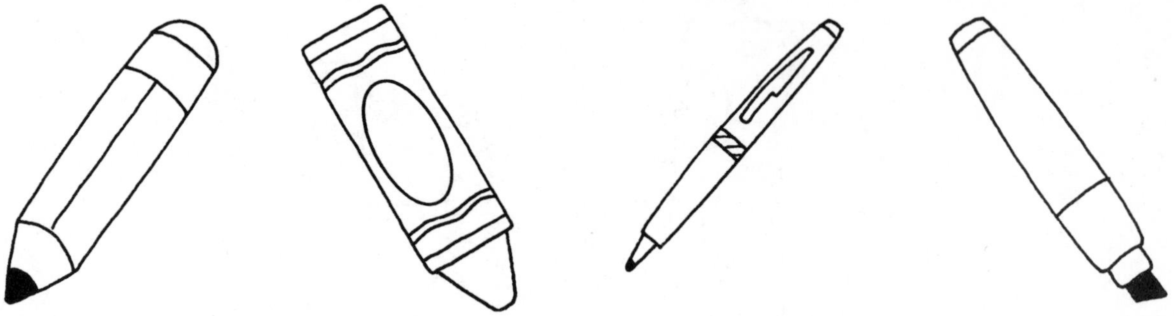

2

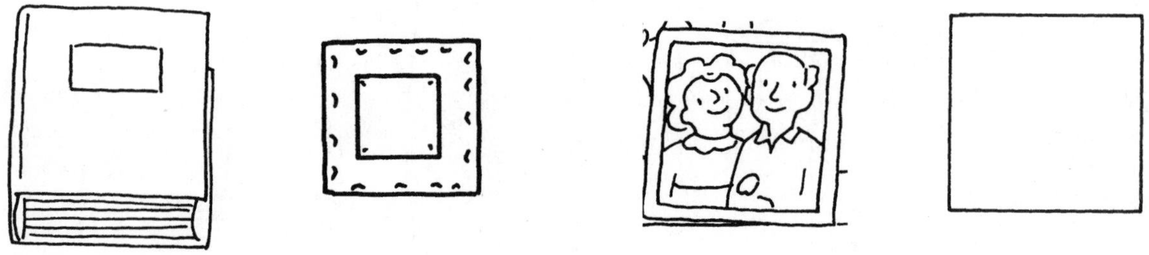

3

4

Directions: Cross out the item that does not belong in a group of: **1** thick things, **2** square things, **3** warm things, and **4** furry things.

Use with Teacher's Edition pages 33A–34.

Name ______________________________

Match One to One

Directions: **1–6** Draw lines to match the items one to one.

Use with Teacher's Edition pages 44A–44D.

Name ____________________

Practice 3.2

Same Number

1

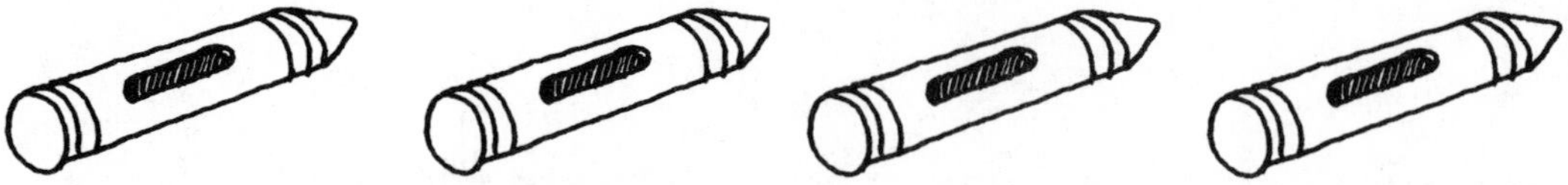

2

3

4

Directions: 1–4 Draw sets to show the same number of items.

Use with Teacher's Edition pages 45A–46.

Name ______________________

Practice 3.3

One and Two

1

2

3

4

5

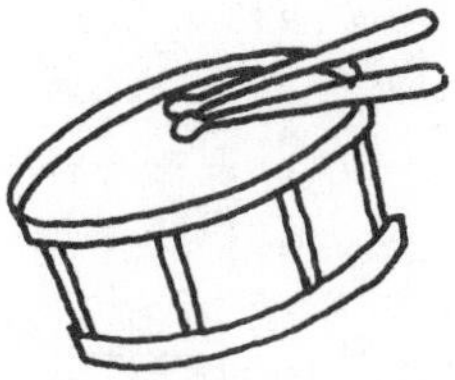
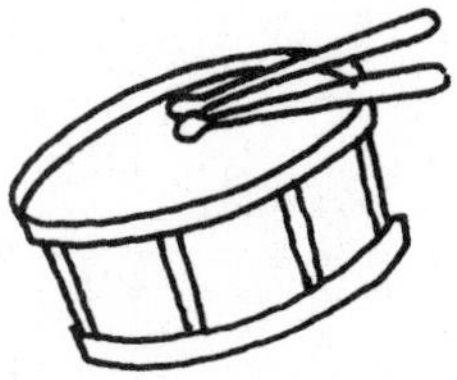

Directions: **1–5** Count the items and write the number.

Use with Teacher's Edition pages 47A–48.

Name ____________________

Three

1

2

3

4

5

6

Directions: 1–6 Count each set and write the number. Then color each set of three.

Use with Teacher's Edition pages 49A–50.

Name ____________________

Four

1

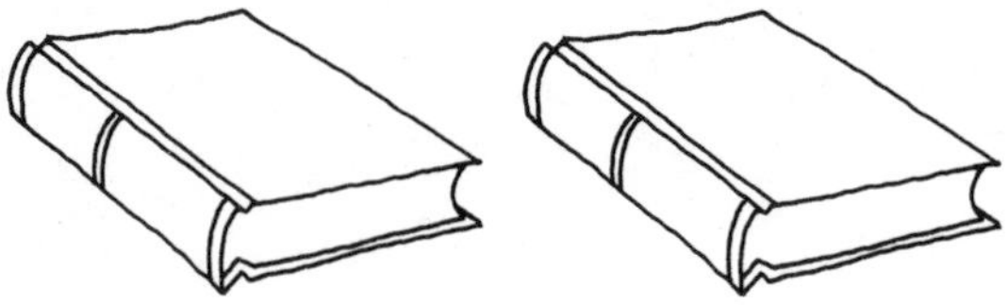

2

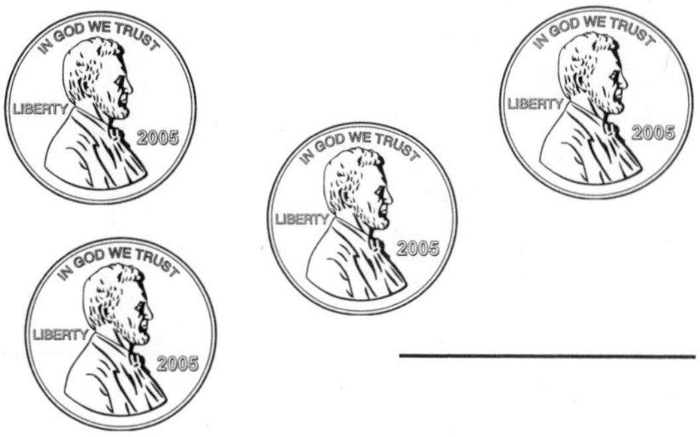

3

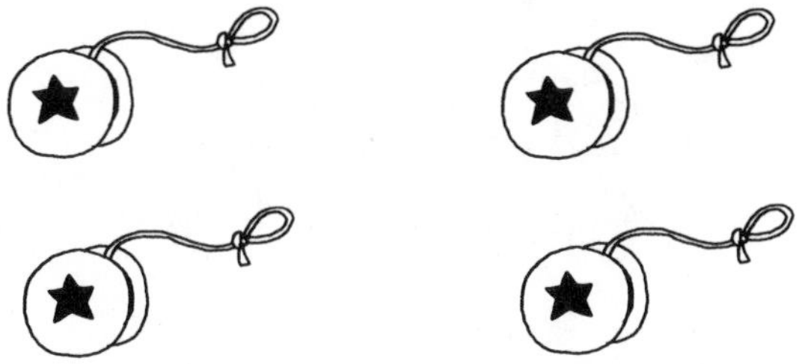

4

5

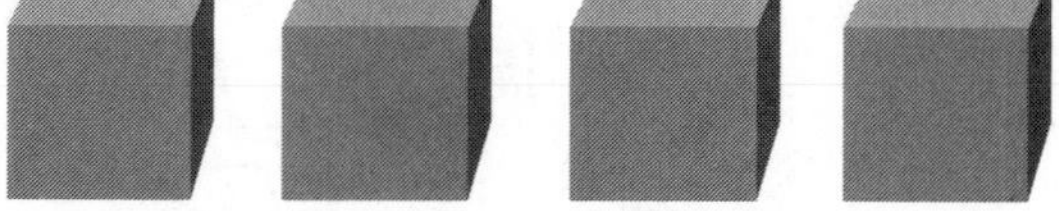

6

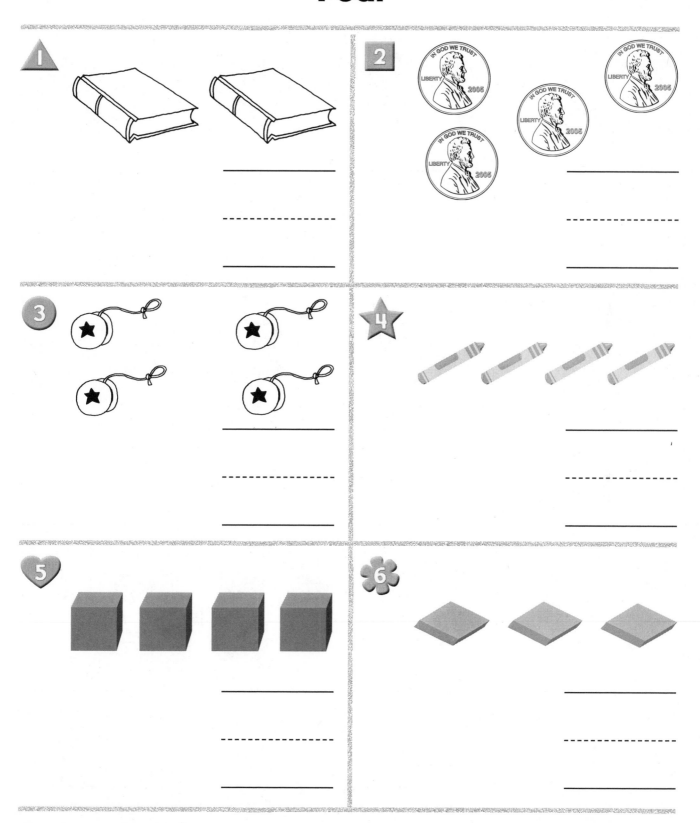

Directions: 1–6 Count each set and write the number. Then color each set of four.

Use with Teacher's Edition pages 51A–52.

Name ______________________________

Five

1

2

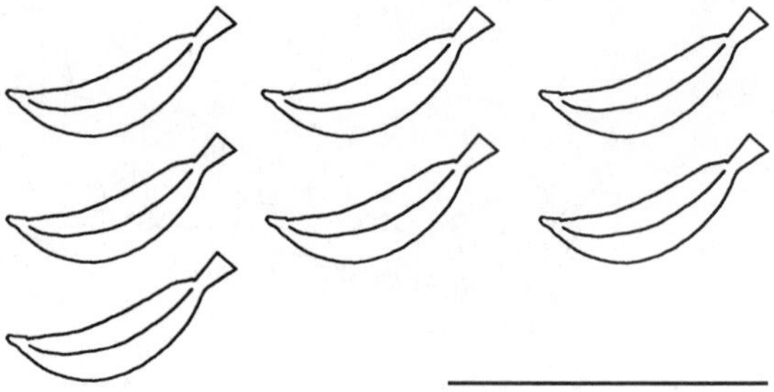

3

4

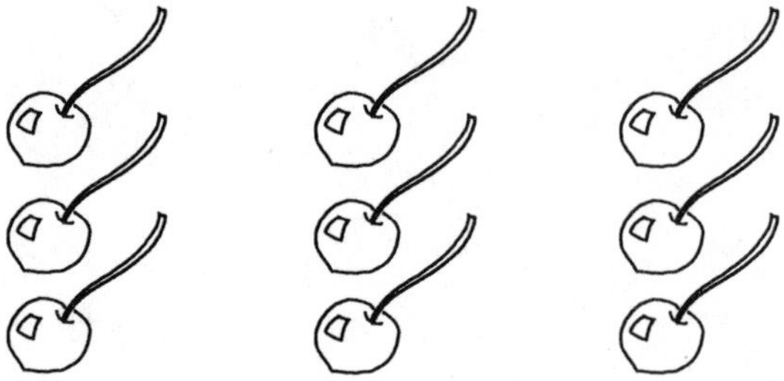

5

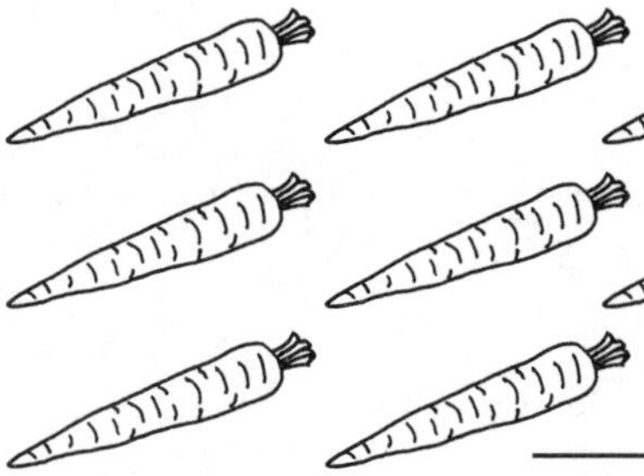

6

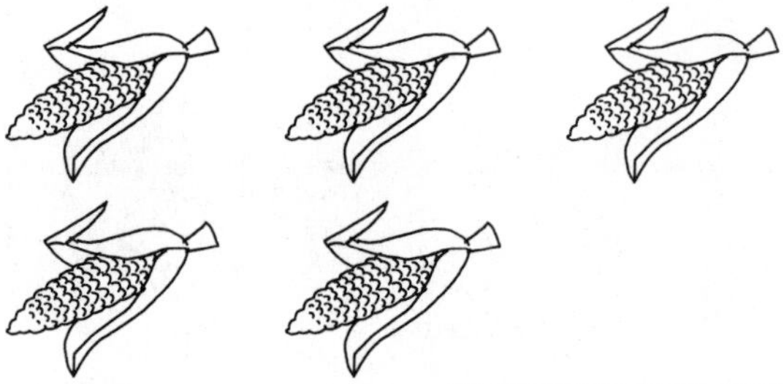

Directions: **1–6** Color five items in the set. Then write the number 5.

Use with Teacher's Edition pages 53A–54.

Name ______________________

Zero

1

0

2

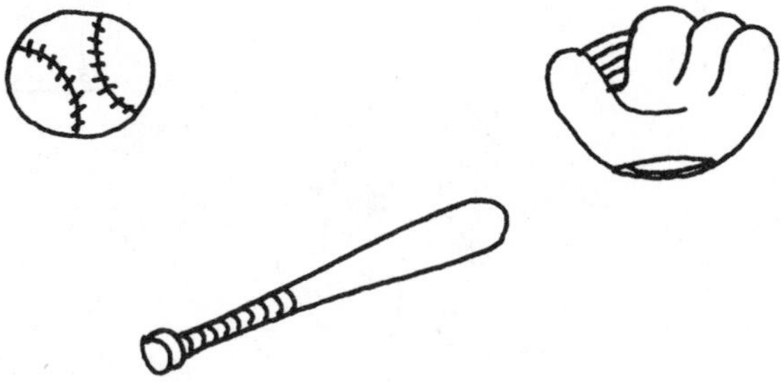

3

4

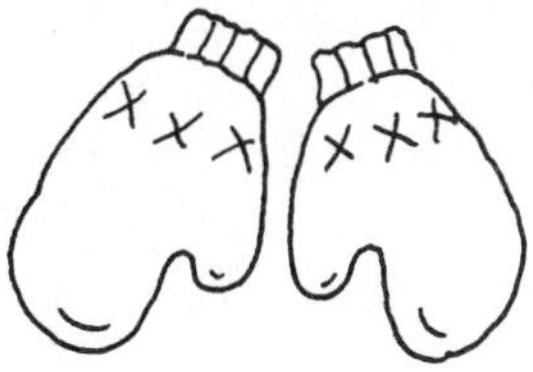

Directions: 1–4 Write how many of the item are in the picture.

Use with Teacher's Edition pages 55A–56.

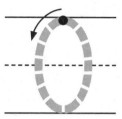

Name ______________________

Using 0–5

1

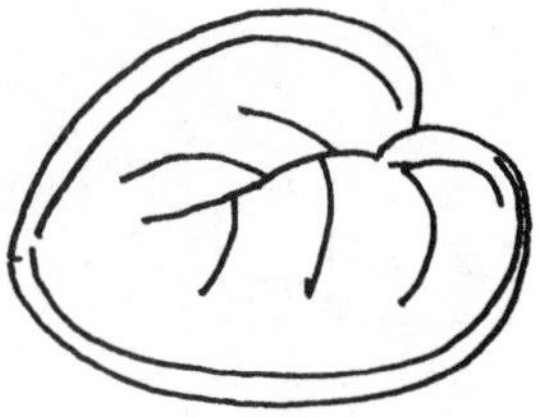

2

3

4

Directions: 1–4 Write the number that shows how many animals.

Use with Teacher's Edition pages 57A–58.

Name ______________________________

Practice 3.9

Problem Solving: Use Logical Reasoning

1

1 2 3 4 5

2

1 2 3 4 5

3

0 1 2 3 4 5

4

0 1 2 3 4 5

Directions: Listen to each clue. Cross out what does not match. Circle what matches all the clues. **1** It is after 3. It is NOT 5. **2** It is between 2 and 4. **3** It is before 2. It is NOT 1. **4** It is between 0 and 2.

Use with Teacher's Edition pages 59A–60.

Name ___________________________________

Practice 3.10

Ordinal Numbers

1

2

3

4

Directions: **1** Circle the third kitten. **2** Circle the second mouse. **3** Circle the fourth frog. **4** Circle the first fish.

Use with Teacher's Edition pages 61A–62.

Name ____________________

More

1

2

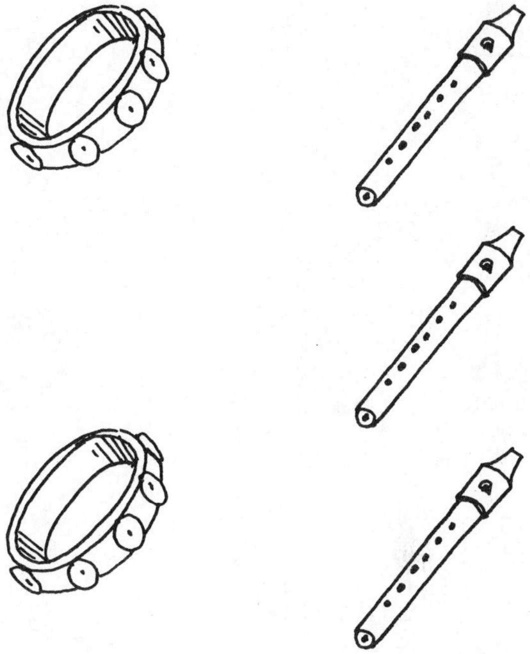

3

4

Directions: 1–4 Count the items in each set. Color the set that has more.

Use with Teacher's Edition pages 67A–68.

Name ____________________

Fewer

1

2

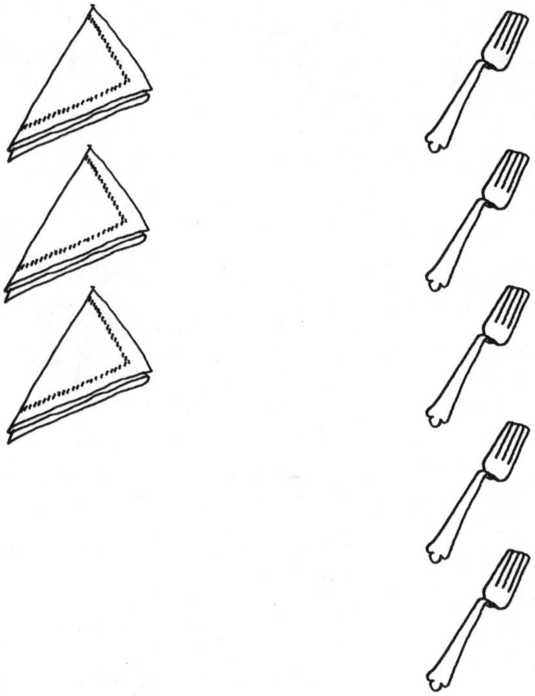

3

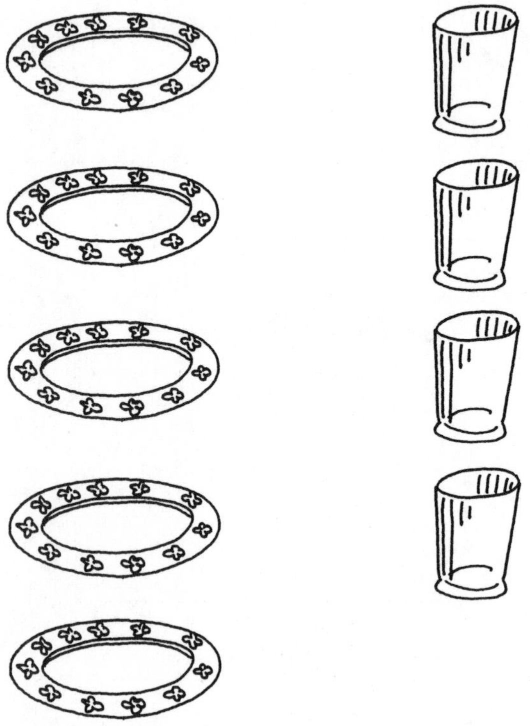

4

Directions: 1–4 Match the items one to one. Circle the set that has fewer.

Use with Teacher's Edition pages 69A–70.

Name ______________________________

Sort and Graph

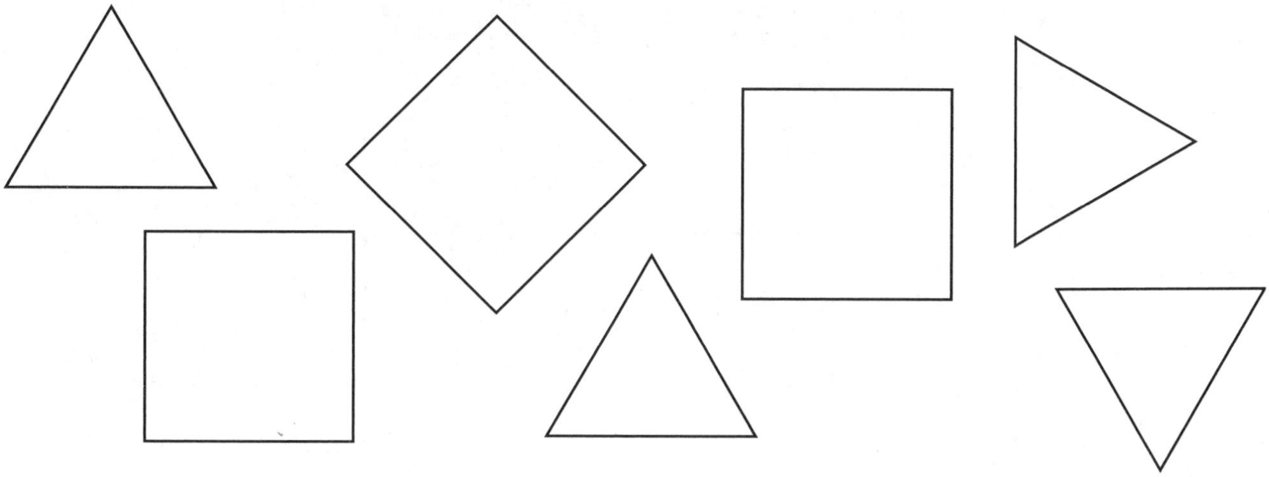

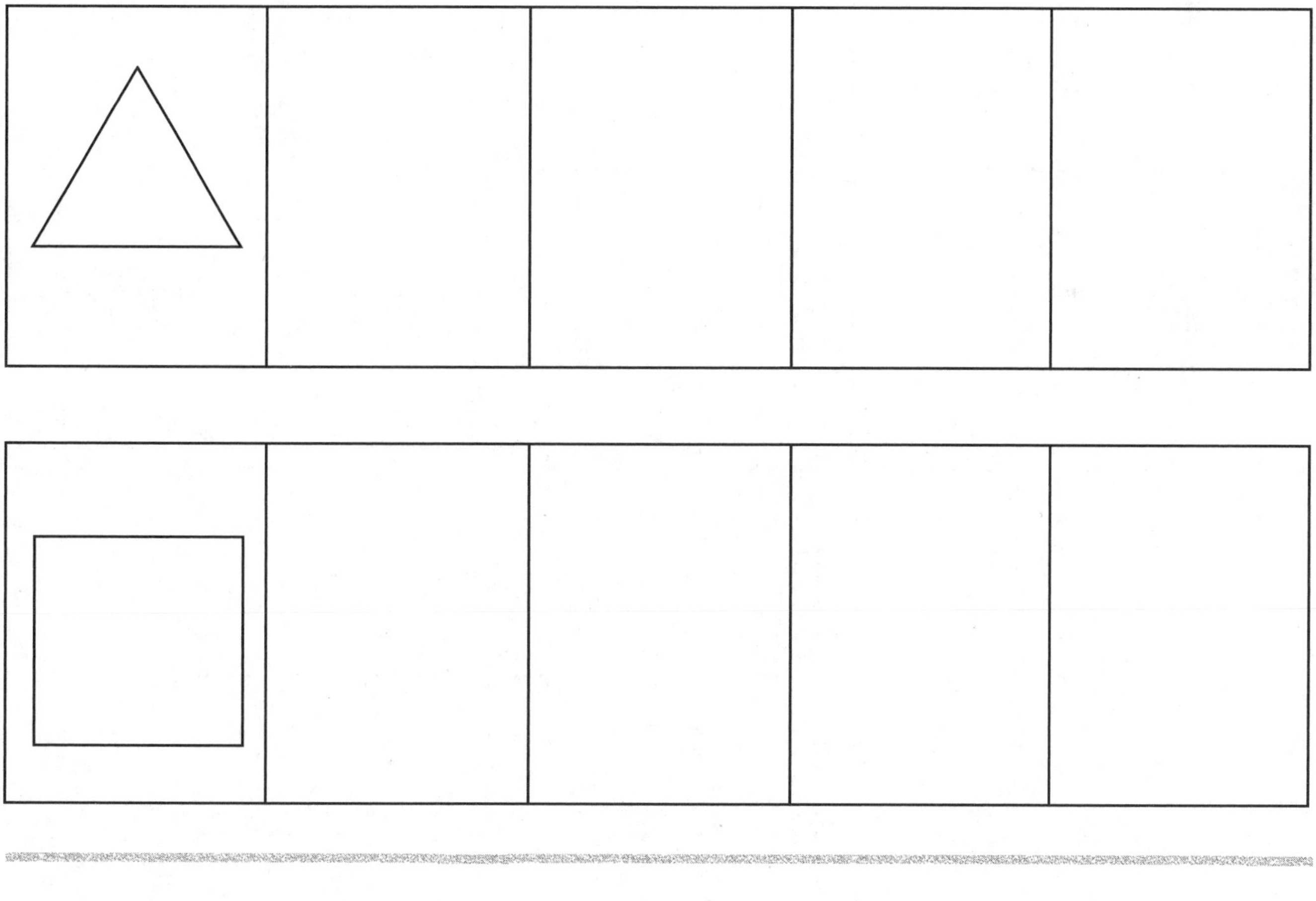

Directions: Place a matching pattern block on each shape above. Sort the blocks by shape. Move the blocks to the graph. Draw or trace the shapes to show your graph.

Use with Teacher's Edition pages 70A–70D.

Name ____________________

Make a Real Graph

How Many of Each?

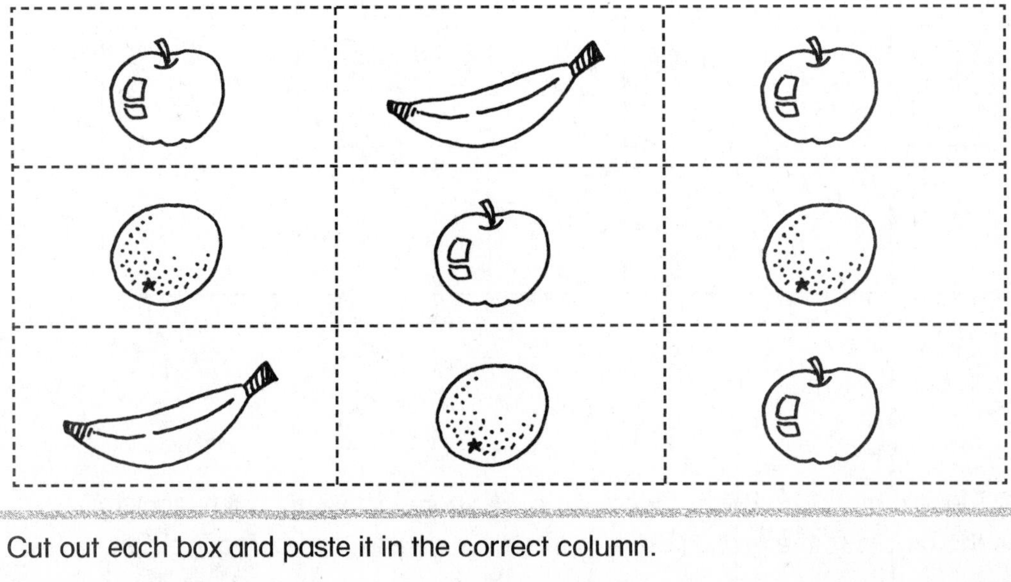

Directions: Cut out each box and paste it in the correct column.

Name ______________________________________

Practice 4.5

Pictographs

How Many?

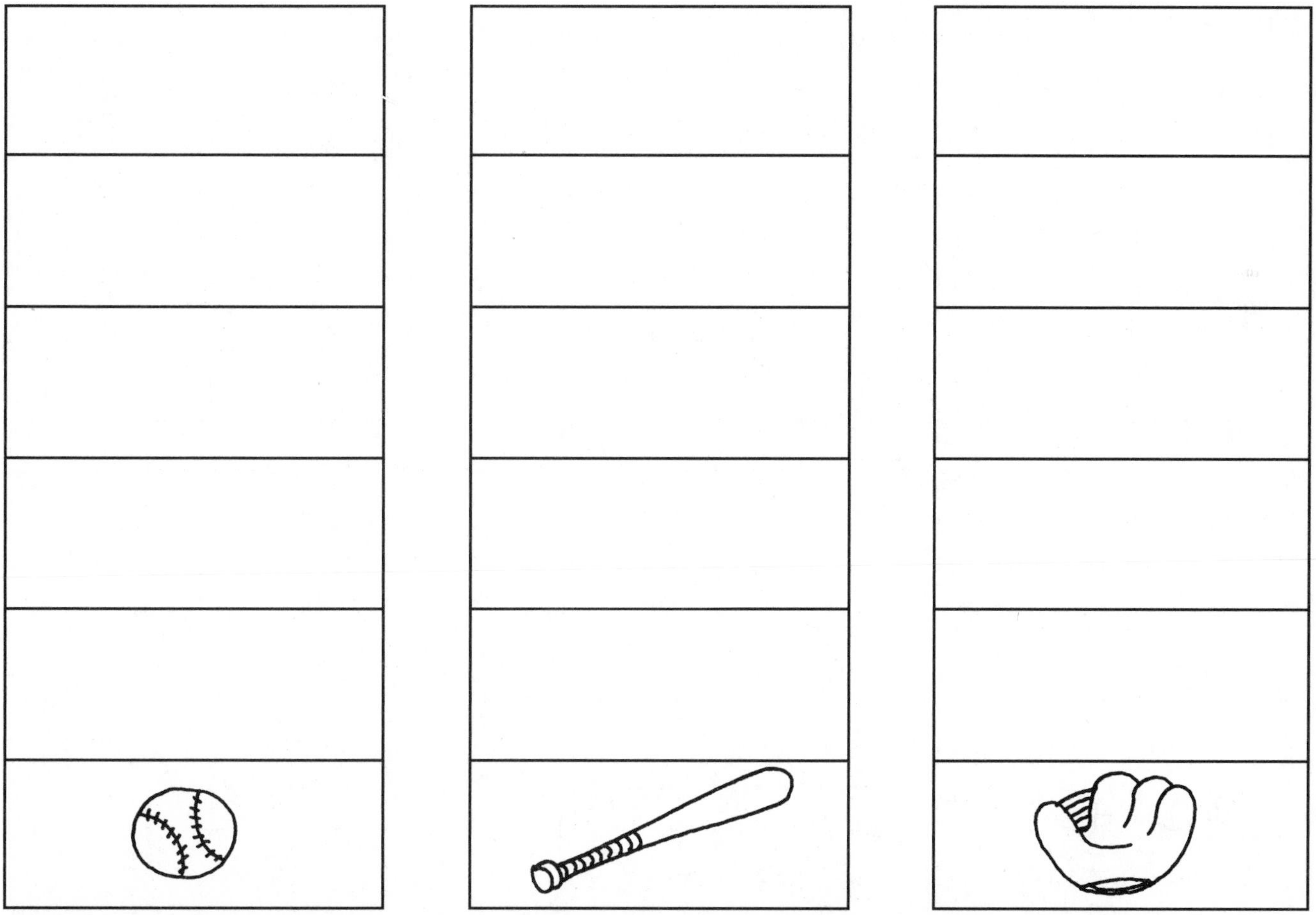

Directions: Count the items in the picture. Color the graph to show how many of each item you counted.

Use with Teacher's Edition pages 71A–72.

Name ____________________

Practice 4.6

Problem Solving: Use a Graph

Ways to Get to School

Directions: Look at the picture. Color the graph to show how each child in the picture gets to school.

Use with Teacher's Edition pages 73A–74.

Name ____________________

Practice 5.1

Circle and Rectangle

1

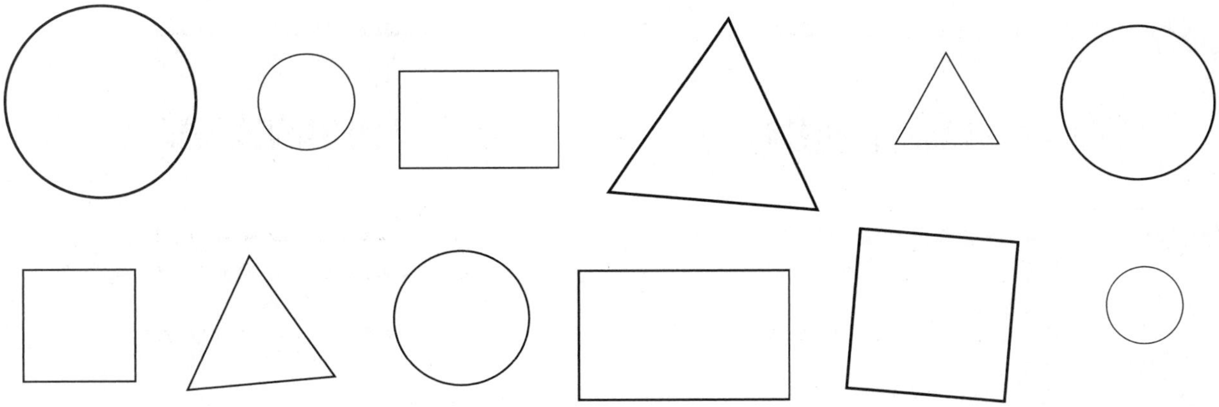

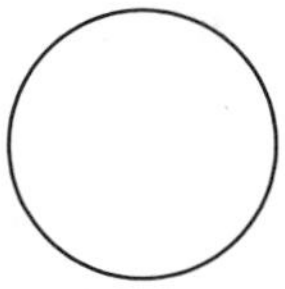

2

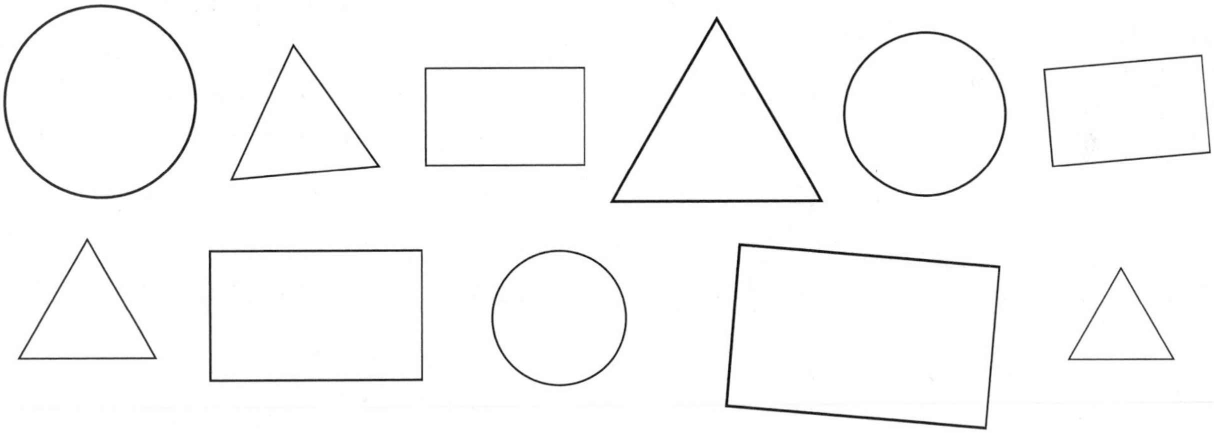

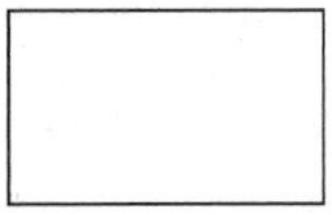

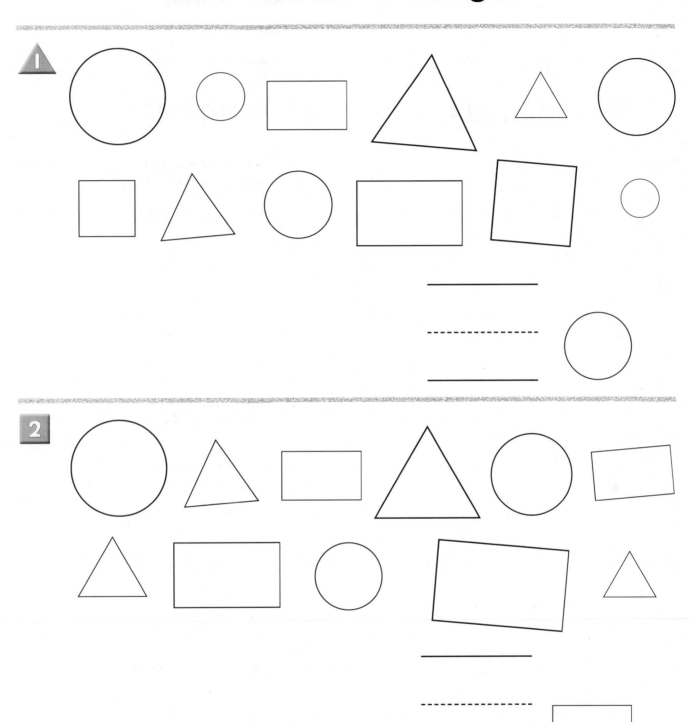

Directions: **I** Color the circles yellow. Write the number. **2** Color the rectangles green. Write the number.

Use with Teacher's Edition pages 85A–86.

Name ____________________

Square and Triangle

1

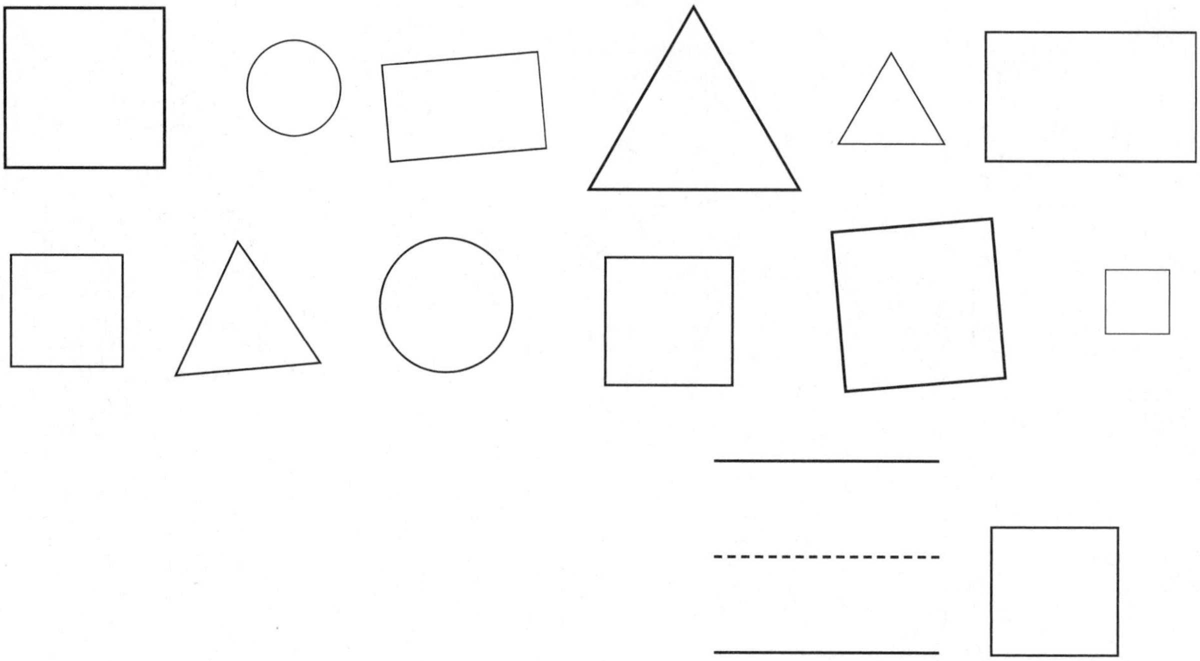

2

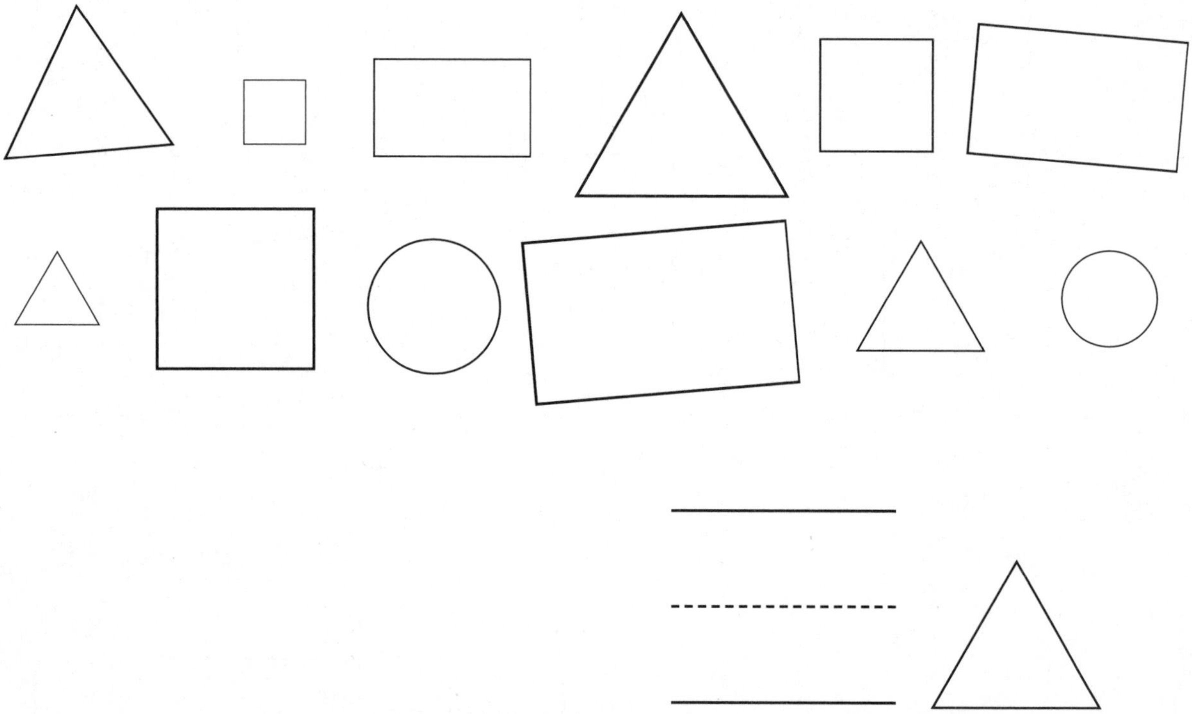

Directions: **1** Color the squares yellow. Write the number. **2** Color the triangles blue. Write the number.

Name ____________________

Patterns With Shapes and Positions

1

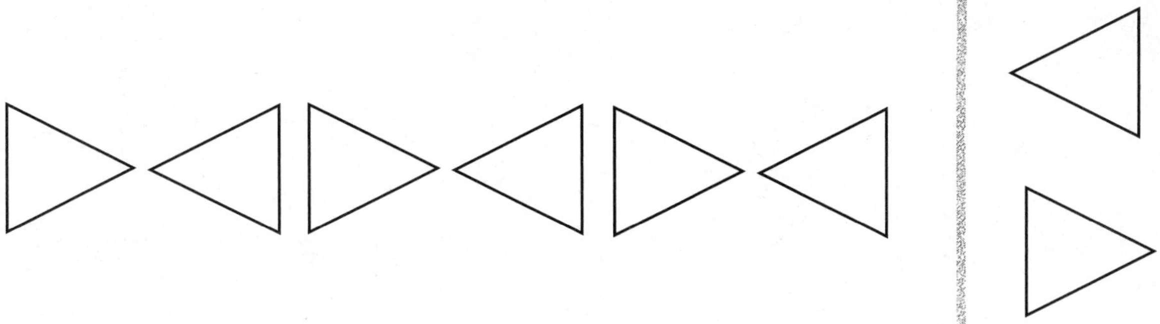

2

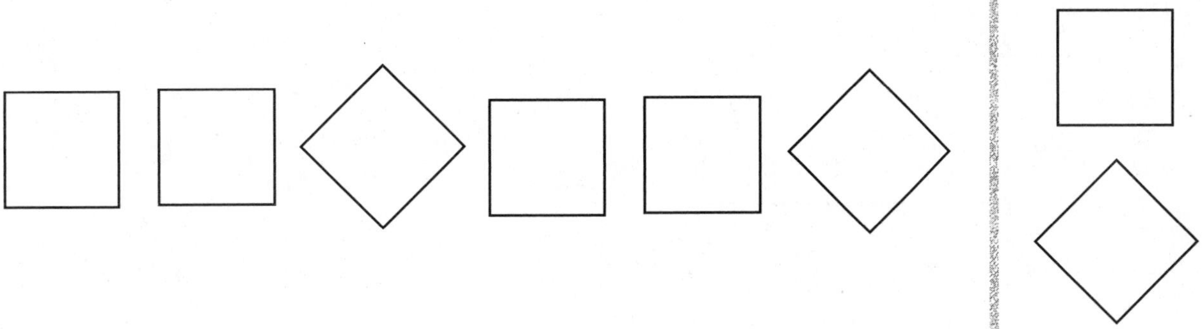

3

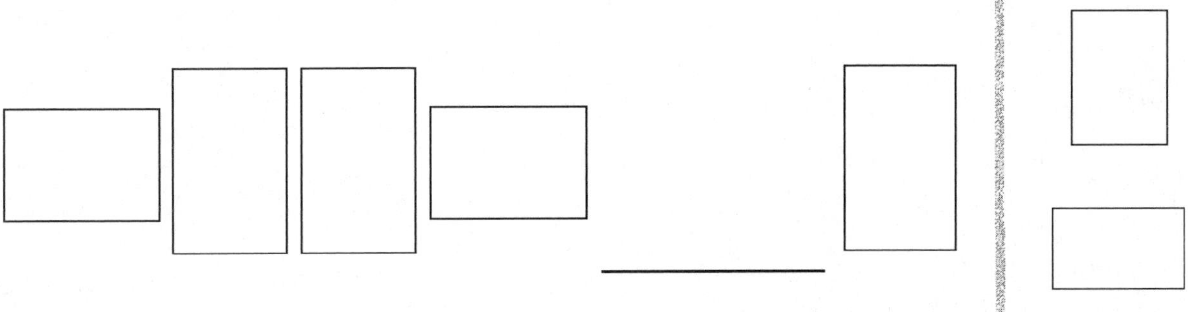

4

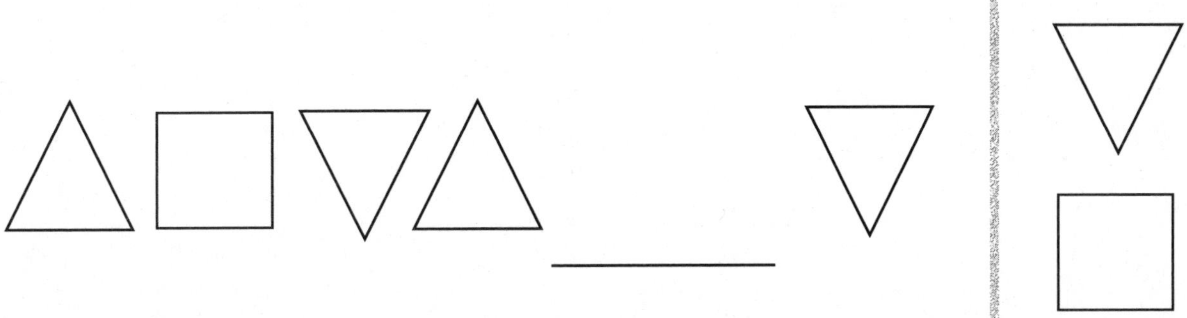

Directions: **1–2** Circle the shape that is likely to come next. **3–4** Circle the missing shape.

Use with Teacher's Edition pages 89A–90.

Name ____

Combine Plane Shapes

1

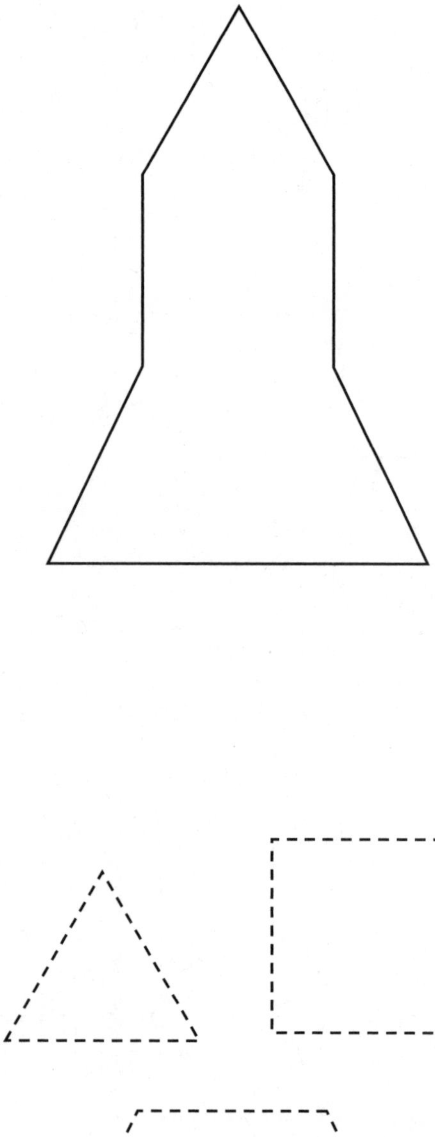

2

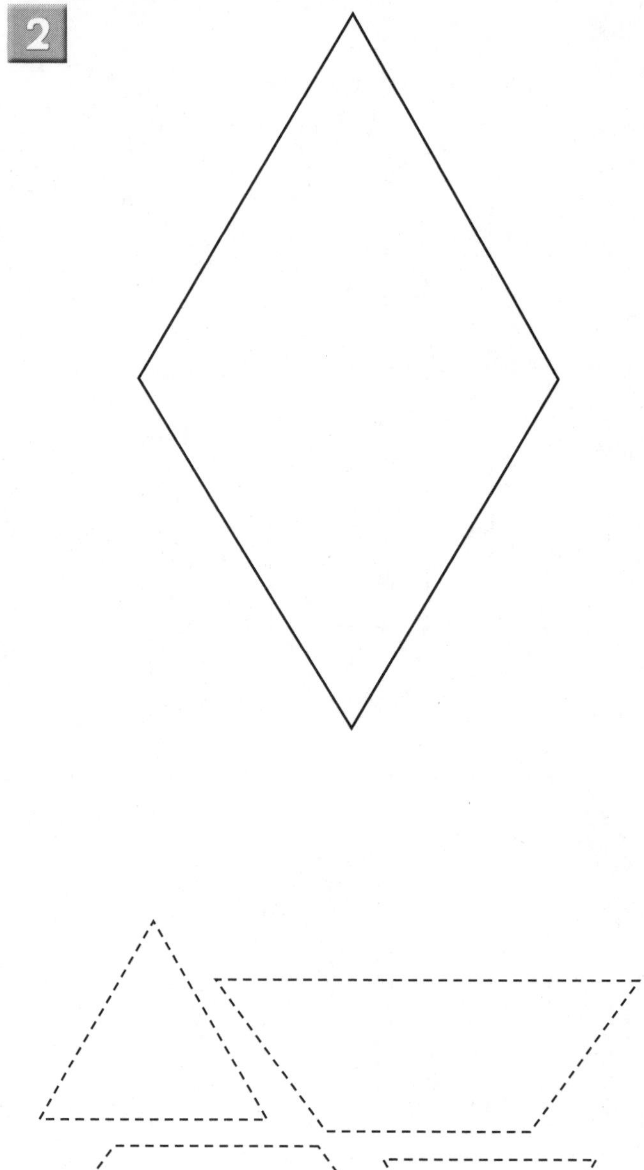

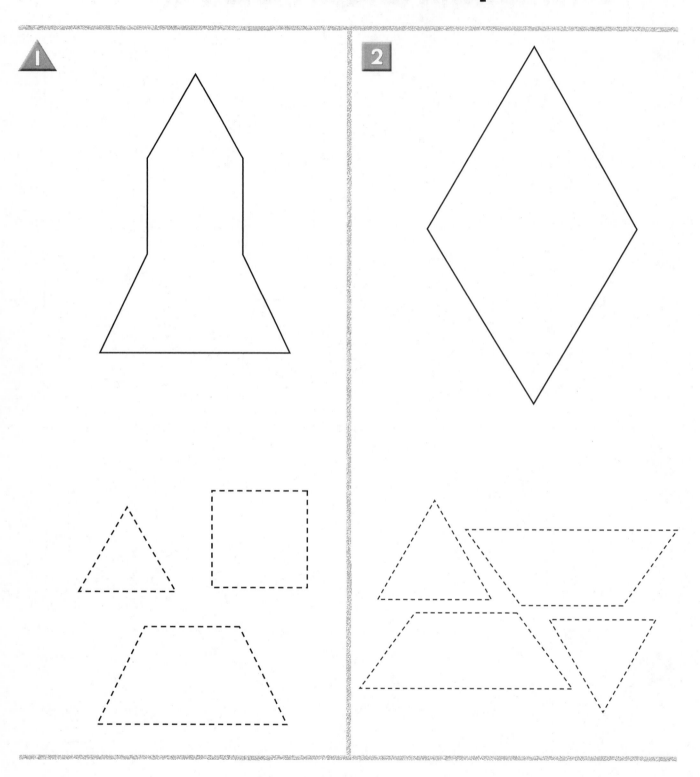

Directions: 1–2 Cut out the shapes. Combine them to make each figure. Paste them to show the shape.

Use with Teacher's Edition pages 90A–90D.

Name ____________________

Practice 5.5

Symmetry

1

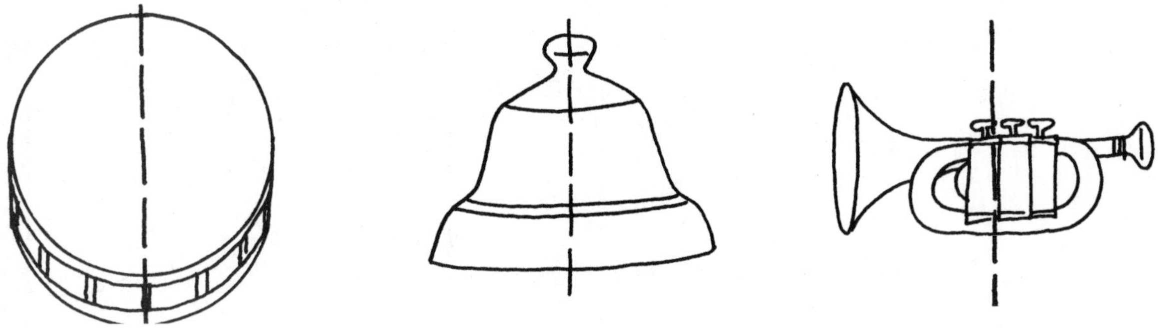

2

3

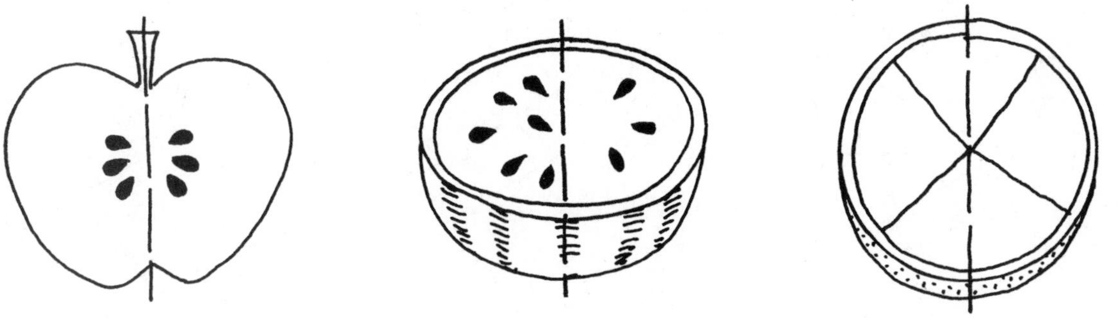

4

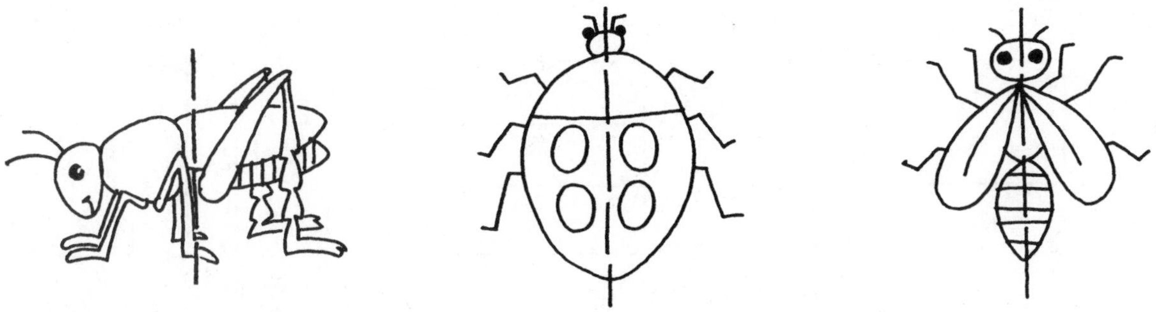

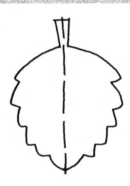

Directions: 1–4 Circle the ones with symmetry.

Use with Teacher's Edition pages 91A–92.

Name ______________________________

Equal Parts

1

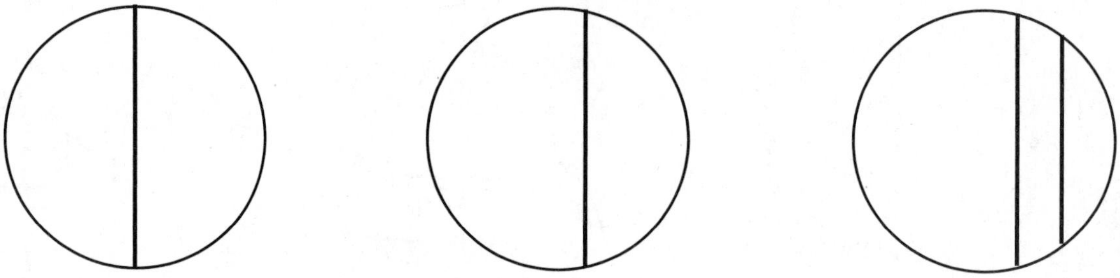

2

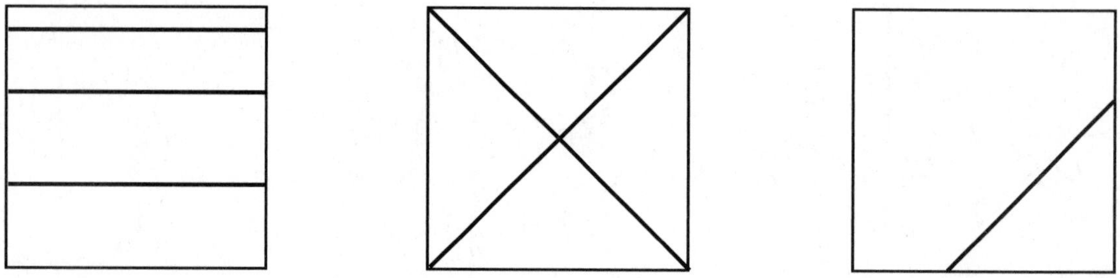

3

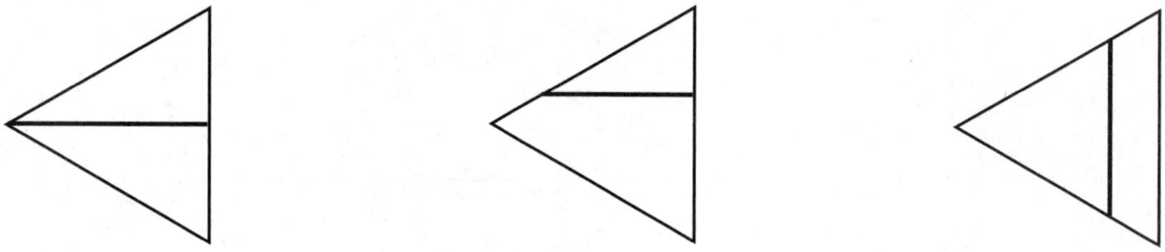

4

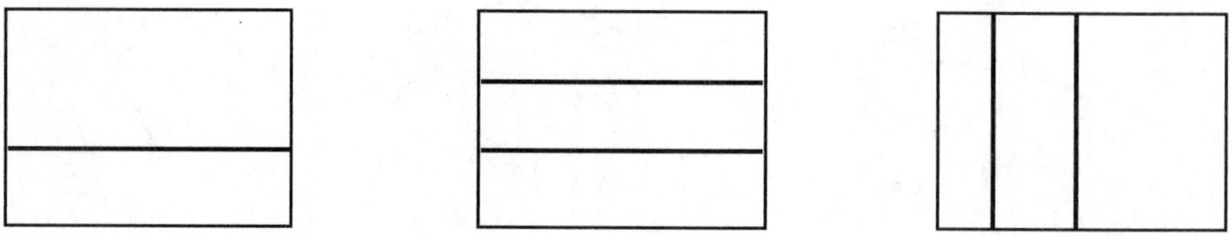

Directions: 1–4 Circle the one that shows equal parts.

Use the Teacher's Edition pages 93A–94.

Name ________________________________

Halves

Directions: Circle the foods that show halves.

Use with Teacher's Edition pages 95A–96.

Name ______________________________

Practice 5.8

Problem Solving: Use a Picture

1

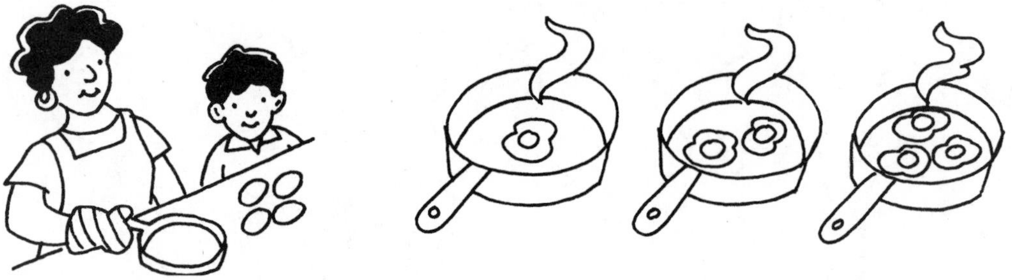

2

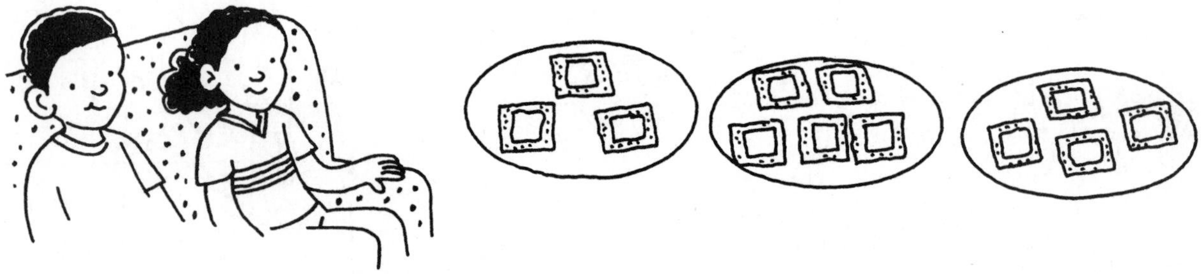

3

4

Directions: 1–4 Count the people shown. Circle the food that would give each person an equal part.

Use with Teacher's Edition pages 97A–98.

Name ______________________________

Likely and Unlikely

1

2

3

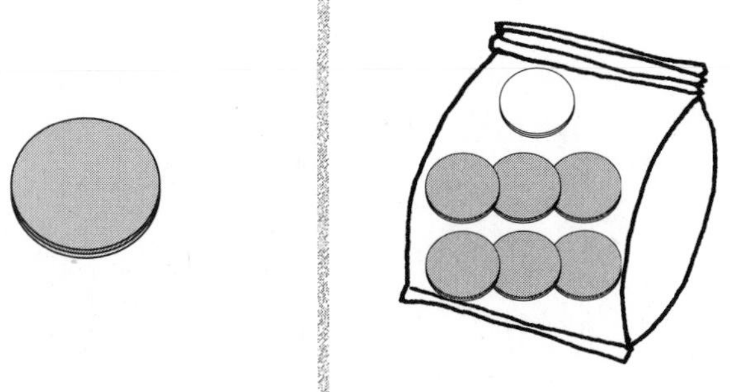

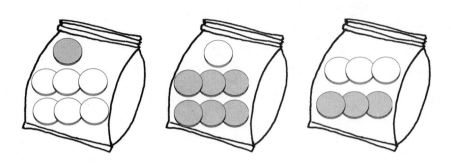

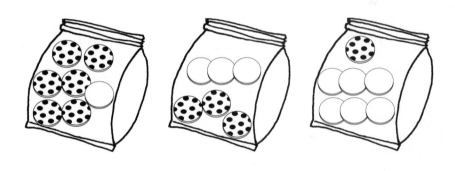

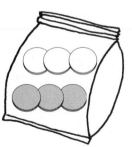

Directions: Circle the bag from which you are **1** most likely to pick a white counter, **2** least likely to pick a dotted counter, and **3** equally likely to pick a gray counter.

Use with Teacher's Edition pages 98A–98D.

Name ______________________

Practice 5.10

Predict and Record Outcomes

Color	Predict	Record
(white)		
(gray)		
(dotted)		

Directions: Predict how many times the spinner will land on each color if you spin five times. Make a tally mark after each spin. Write the numbers of tally marks.

Use with Teacher's Edition pages 99A–100.

Name ______________________________

Sort Solid Shapes

1

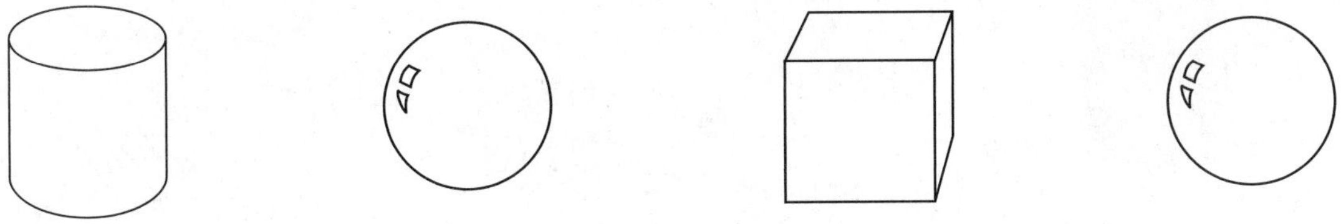

2

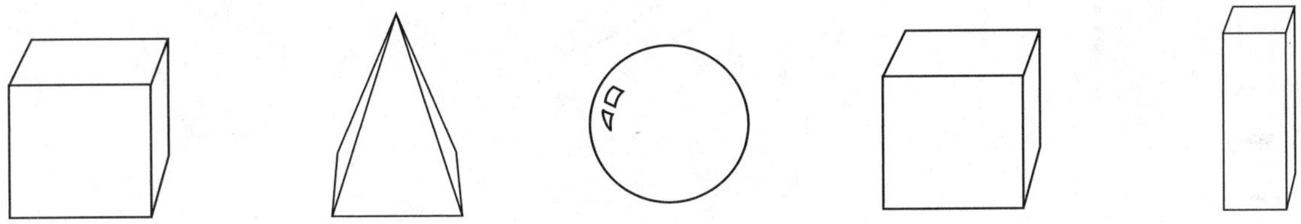

3

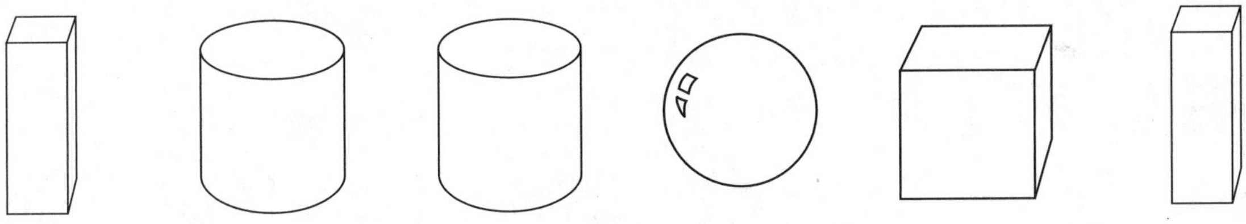

4

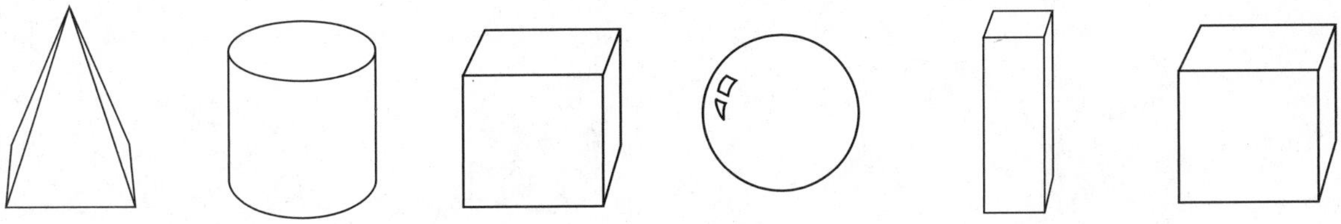

Directions: 1–4 Color the shapes that have corners orange. Color the shapes that have curves green.

Use with Teacher's Edition pages 105A–106.

Name ____________________

Practice 6.2

Identify Solid Shapes

1

2

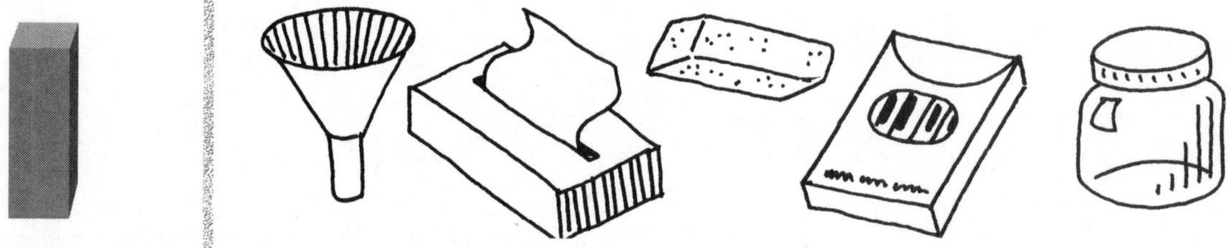

3

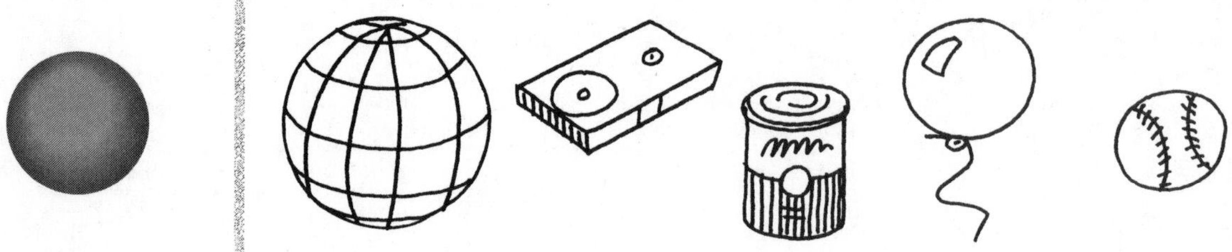

4

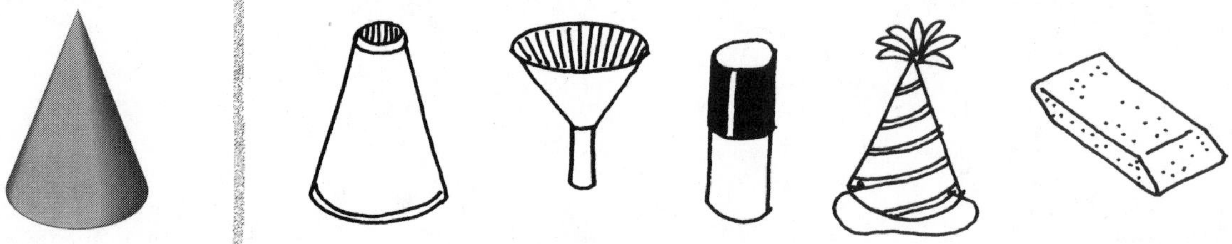

5

Directions: **1–5** Name and describe the solid shapes. Circle the objects that are like the solid shape.

Use with Teacher's Edition pages 107A–108.

Name ____________________

Build Solid Shapes

1

2

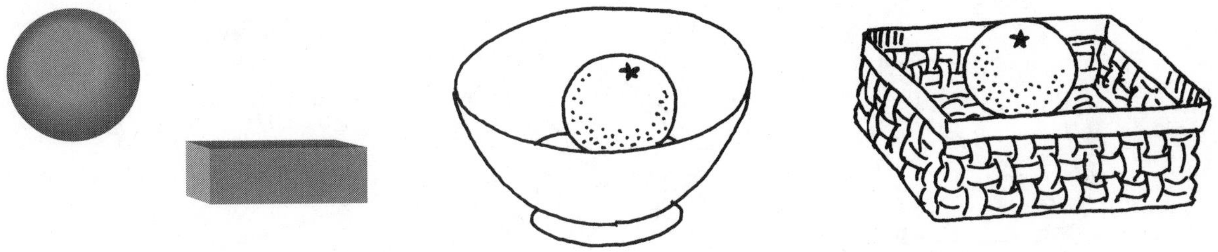

3

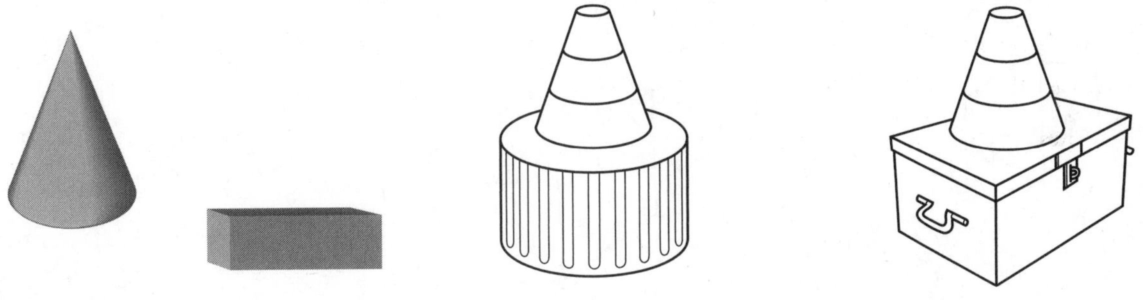

4

Directions: **1–4** Look at the solids. Circle the picture that is made with similar shapes.

Use with Teacher's Edition pages 108A–108D.

Name ______________________________

Surfaces of Solid Shapes

1

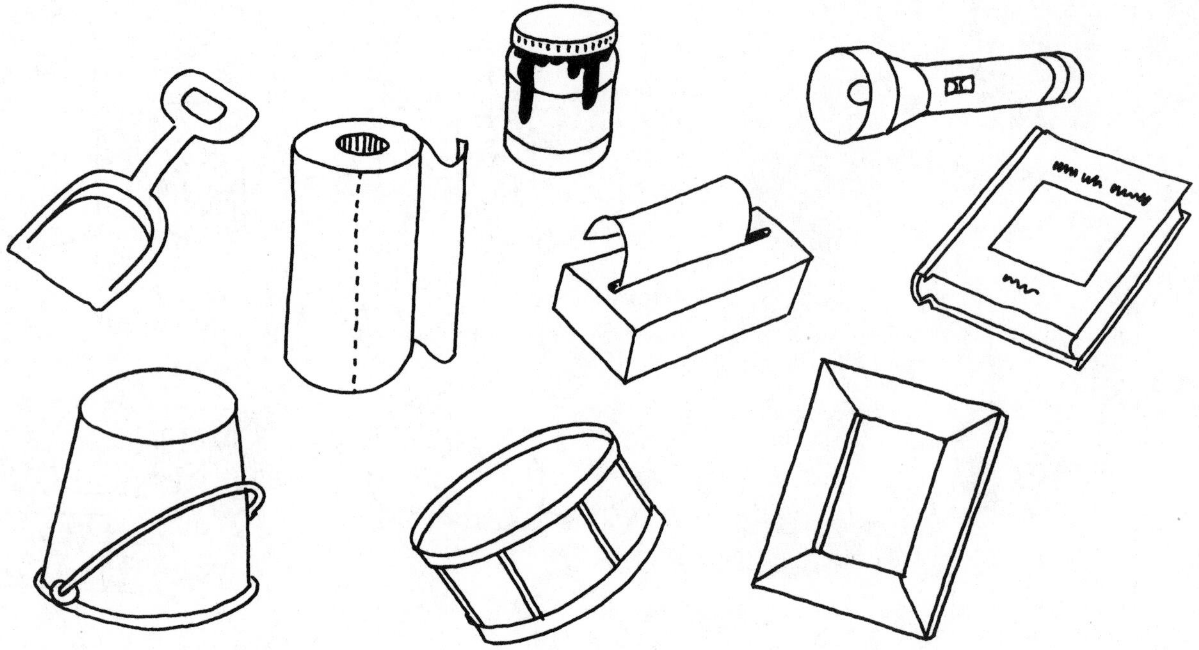

2

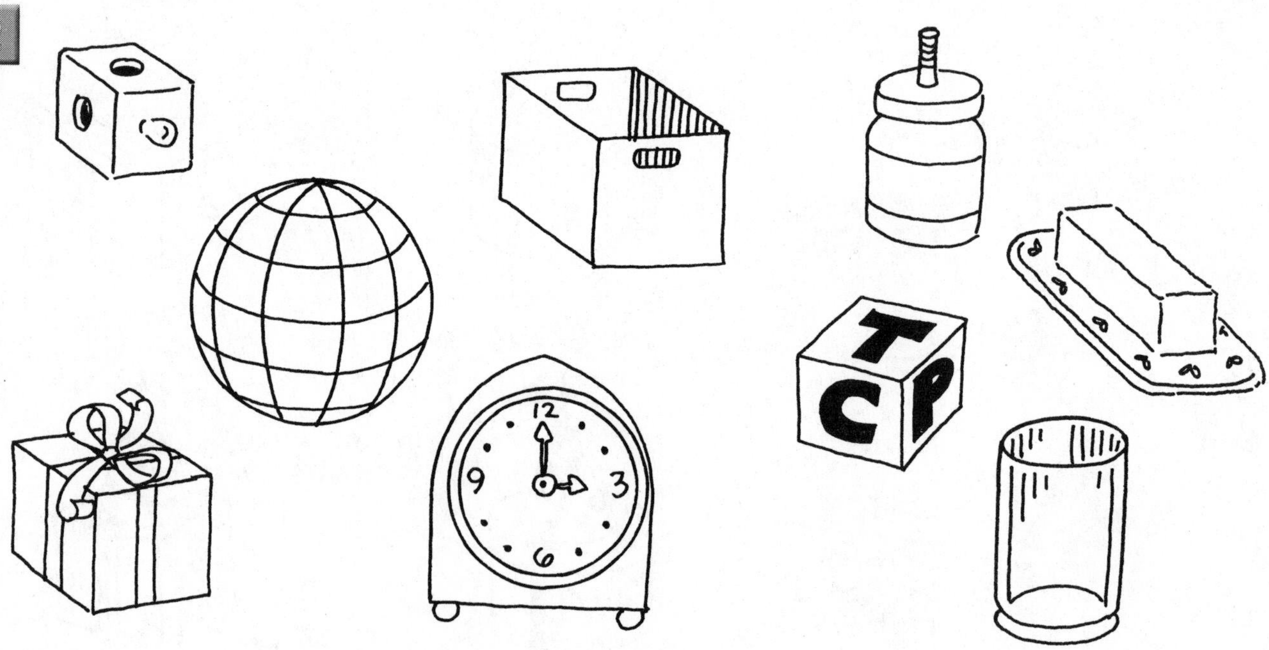

Directions: **1** Circle the shapes that have a circular surface. **2** Circle the shapes that have a square surface.

Use with Teacher's Edition pages 109A–110.

Name ____________________

Combine Solid Shapes

1

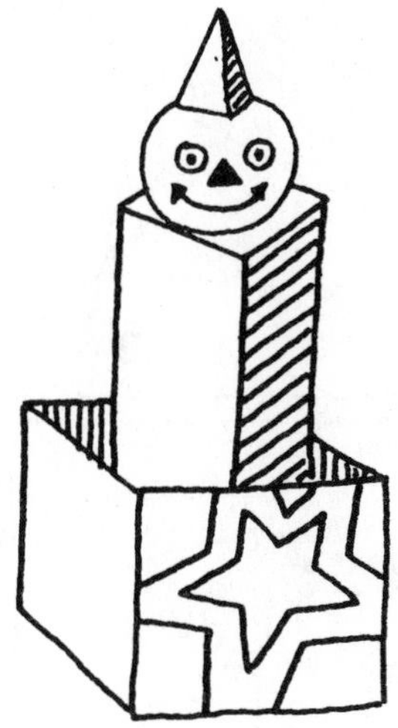

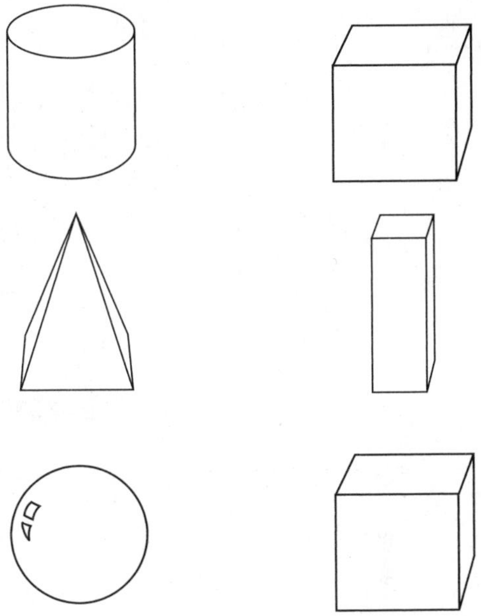

2

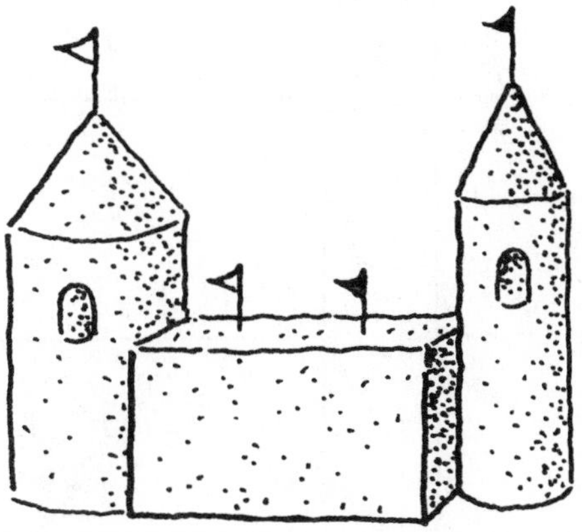

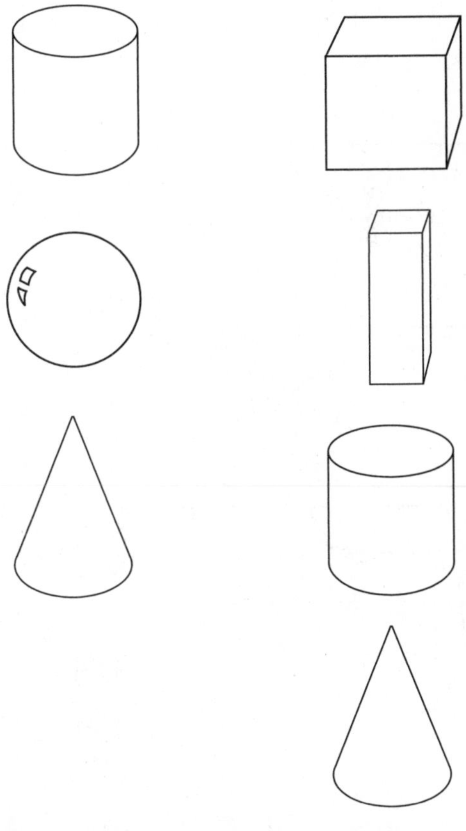

Directions: **1** Color the shapes that were used to make the Jack-in-the-box. **2** Color the kind of shapes that were used to make the sandcastle.

Use with Teacher's Edition pages 111A–112.

Name ______________________________

Problem Solving: Make a Graph

1

How Many Shapes?

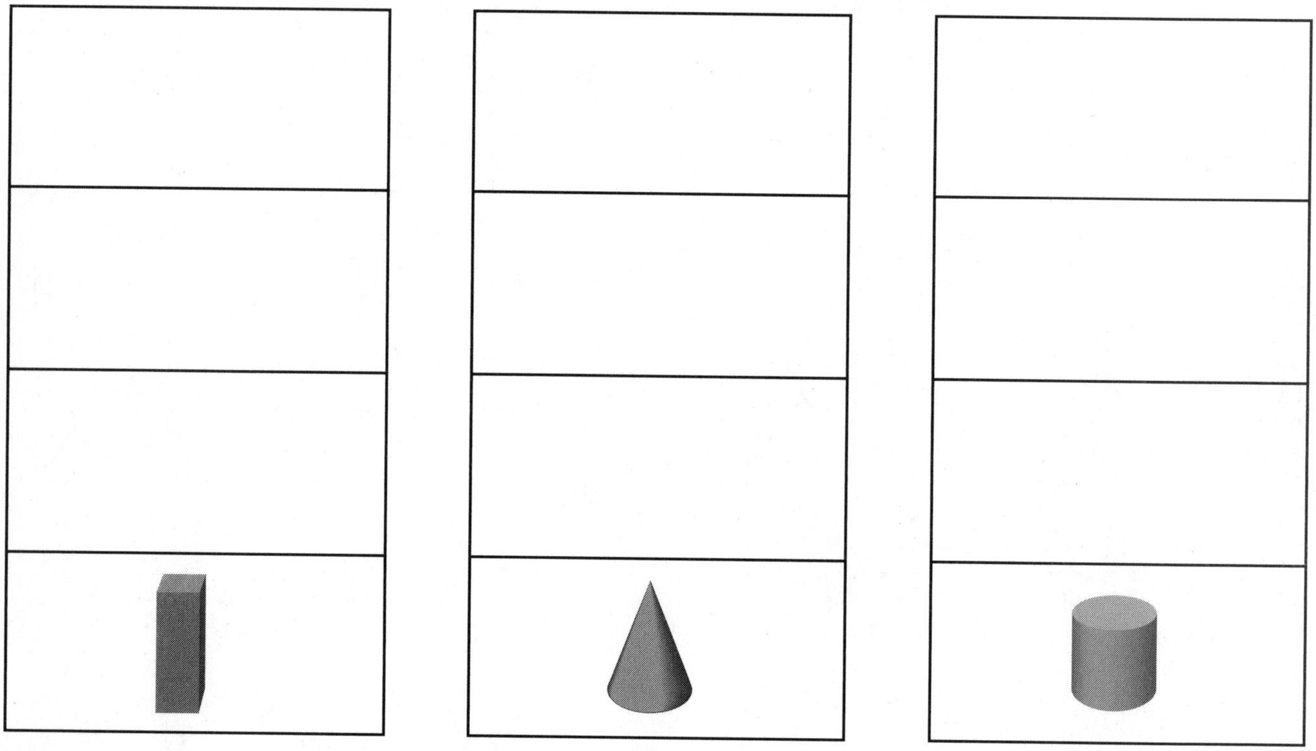

2

______  ______  ______ 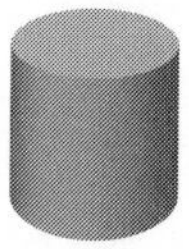

Directions: **1** Color one box in the graph for each item that is like the solid shape.
2 Count the colored boxes and write the numbers. Compare the numbers of shapes.

Name ________________________

Six

1

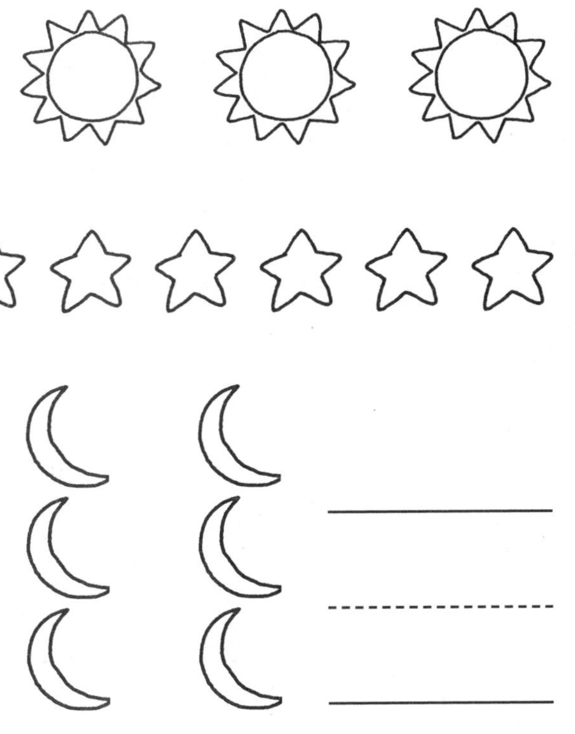

2

3

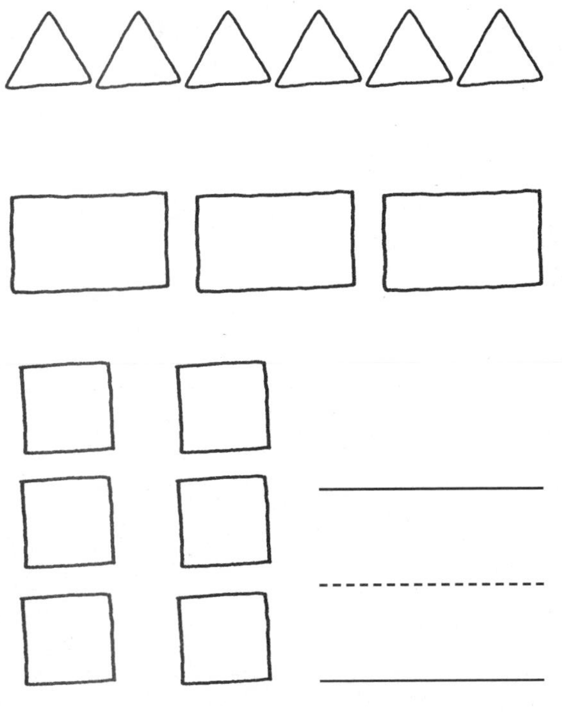

4

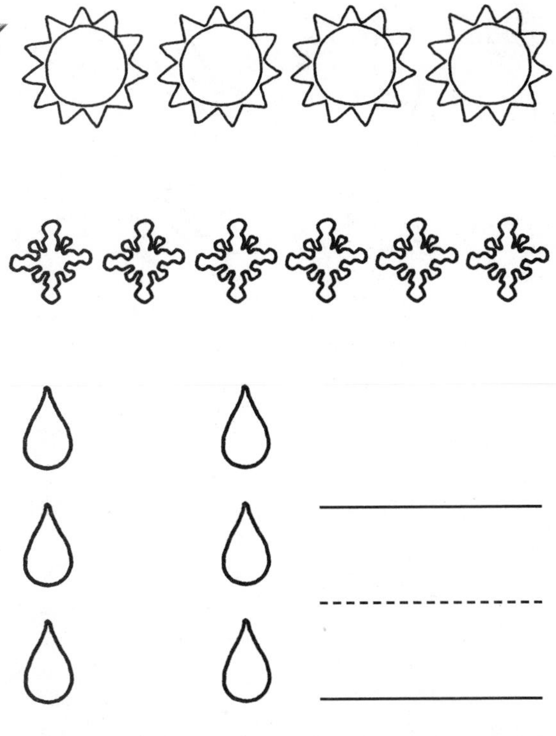

Directions: 1–4 Circle the sets of 6. Write the number.

Use with Teacher's Edition pages 125A–126.

Name ______________________________

Practice 7.2

Seven

1

2

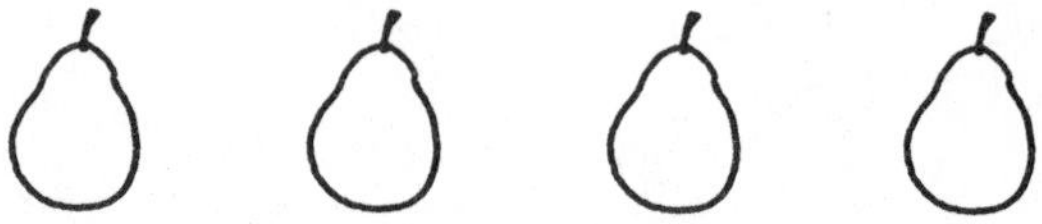

3

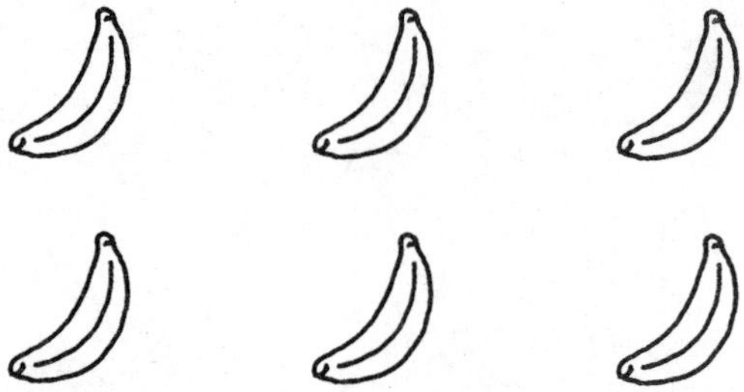

4

Directions: 1–4 Count the items. Draw more to make a set of 7. Write the number.

Use with Teacher's Edition pages 127A–128.

Name ______________________________

Practice 7.3

Eight

1

2

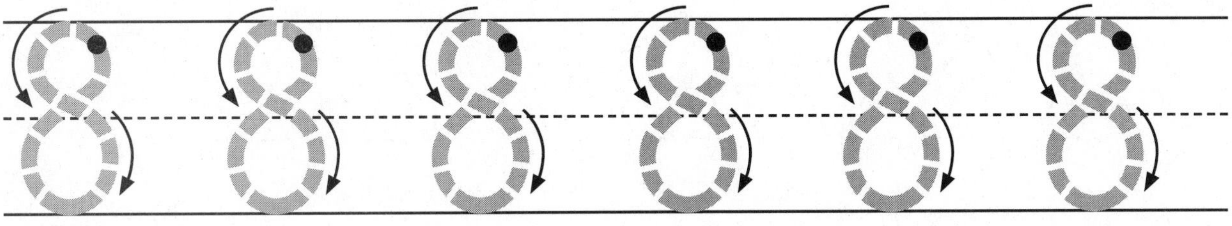

Directions: **1** Circle the groups of 8. **2** Write the number.

Use with Teacher's Edition pages 129A–130.

Name ______________________

Nine

1

______

2

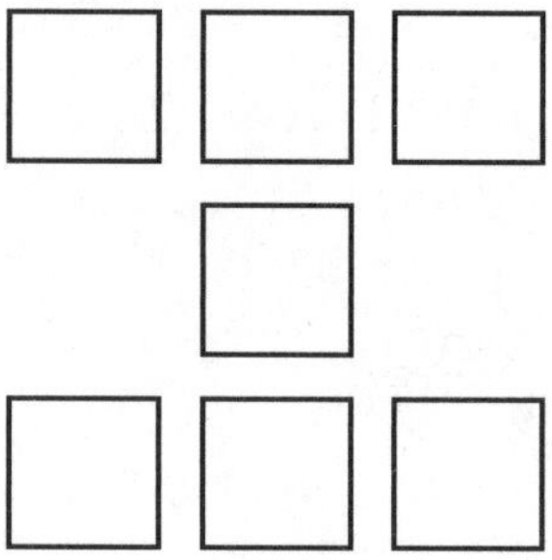

______

3

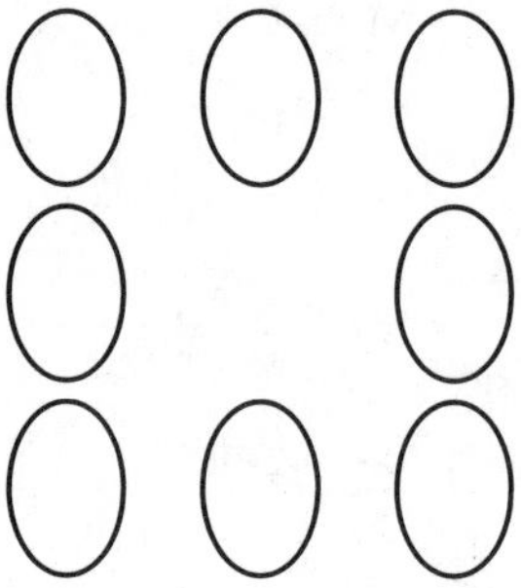

______

4

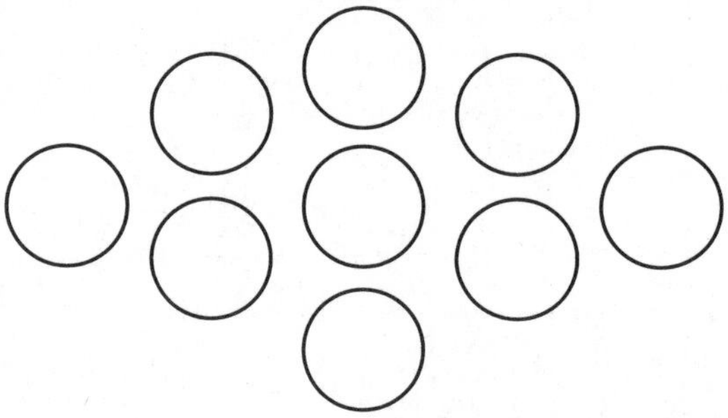

______

5

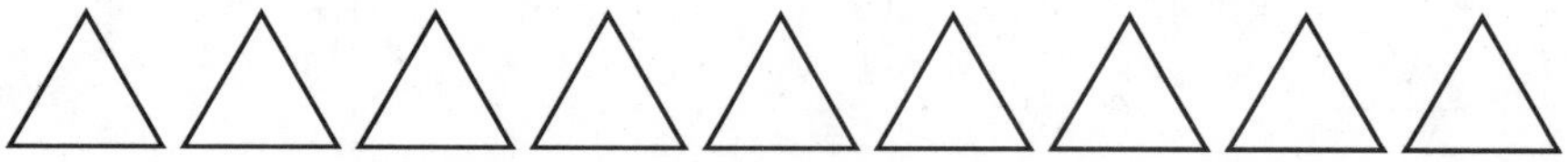

______

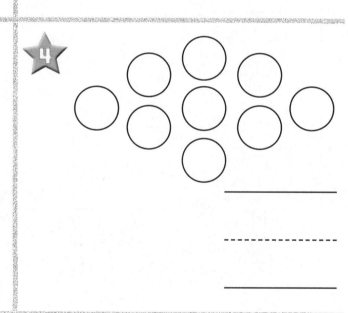

Directions: **1–5** Count the items. Write the number.

Use with Teacher's Edition pages 131A–132.

Name ____________________

Ten

1
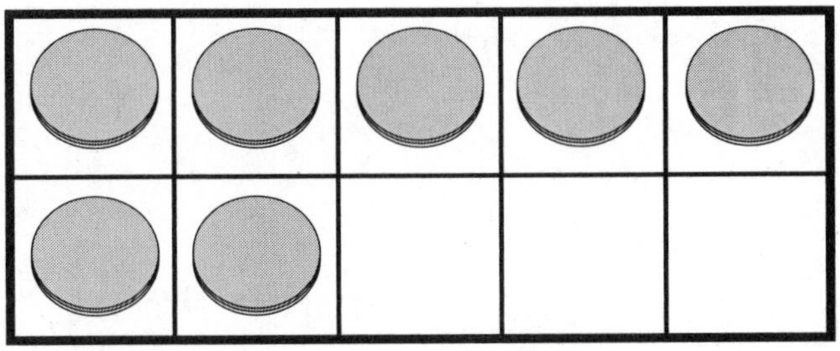

2
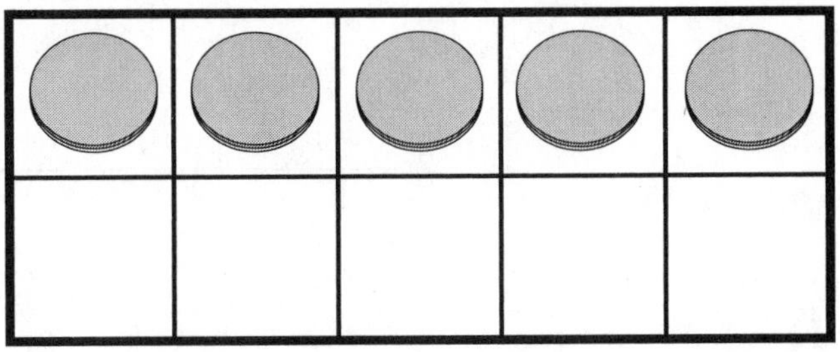

3
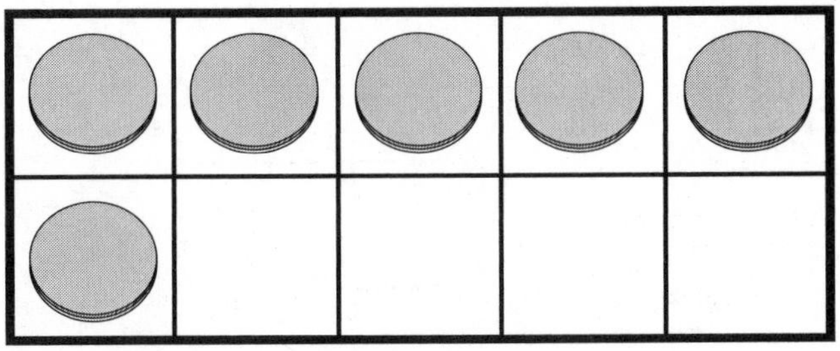

4
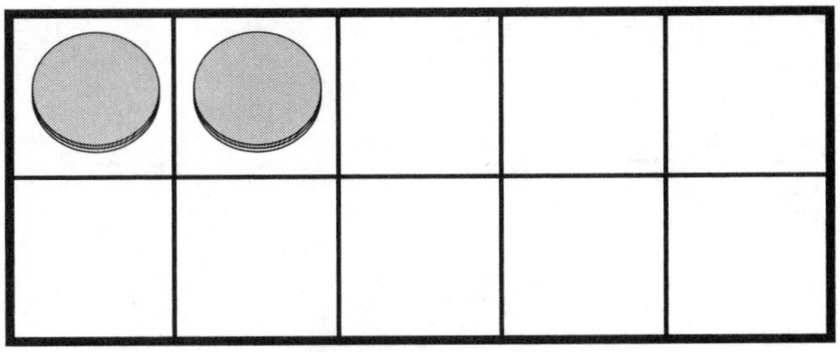

Directions: 1–4 Draw counters in the ten-frame to make 10. Write the number.

Use with Teacher's Edition pages 133A–134.

Name ______________________

Practice 7.6

Problem Solving: Use a Pattern

1

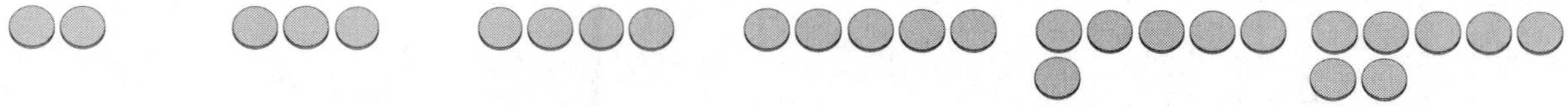

2 3 4 5 ____ ____

2

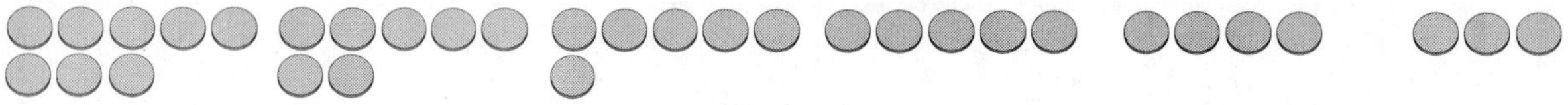

8 7 6 5 ____ ____

3

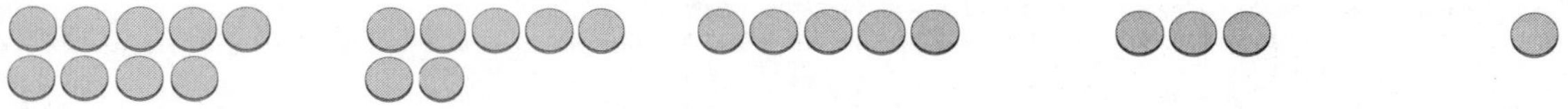

9 7 5 ____ 1

4

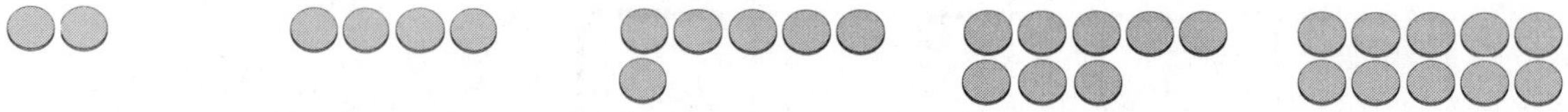

2 4 ____ 8 ____

Directions: 1–4 Count the dots. Look for a pattern. Write the missing number.

Use with Teacher's Edition pages 135A–136.

Name ______________________

Eleven

1

9

10

11

2

9

10

11

3

9

10

11

4

9

10

11

5

9

10

11

Directions: 1–5 Count the items. Circle the number.

Use with Teacher's Edition pages 137A–138.

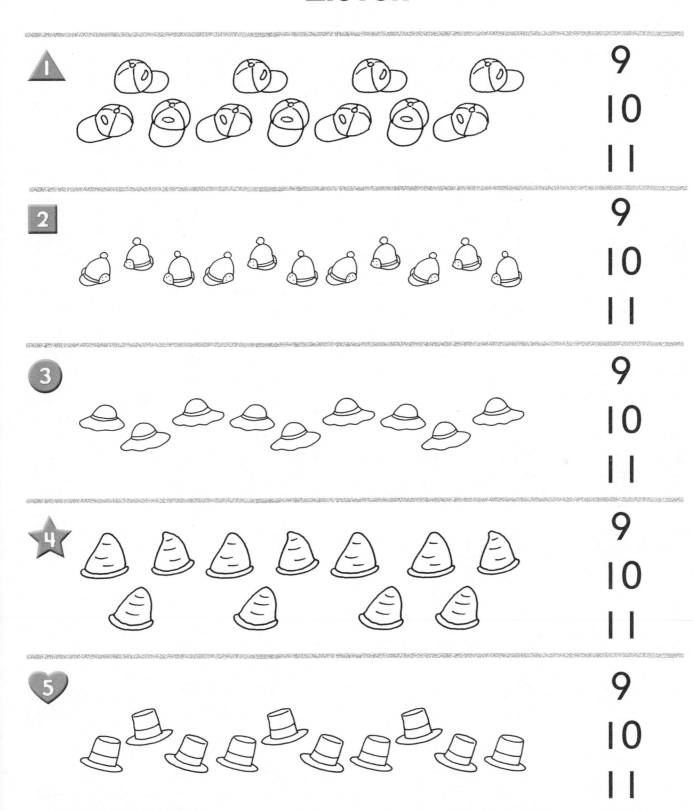

Name ________________________

Practice 7.8

Twelve

1 

2 

3 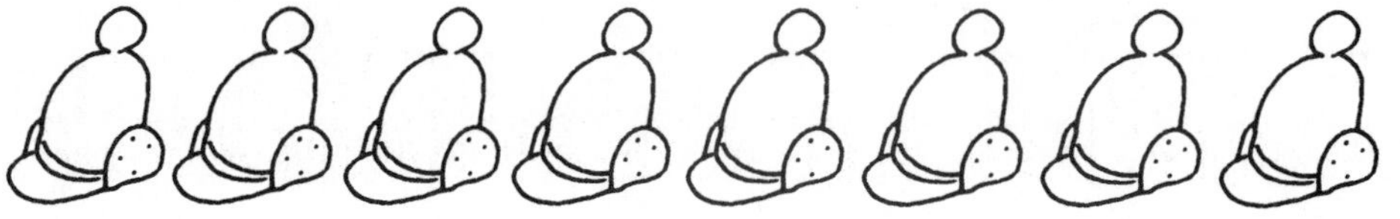

4 

Directions: 1–4 Count the objects. Draw more to make 12. Write the number.

Use with Teacher's Edition pages 139A–140.

Name ______________________

Practice 8.1

Names for 1–12

1

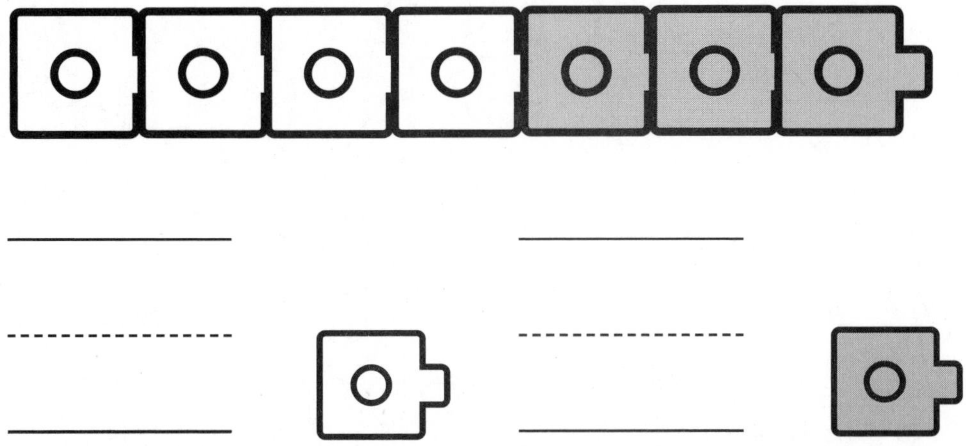

5

6

7

2

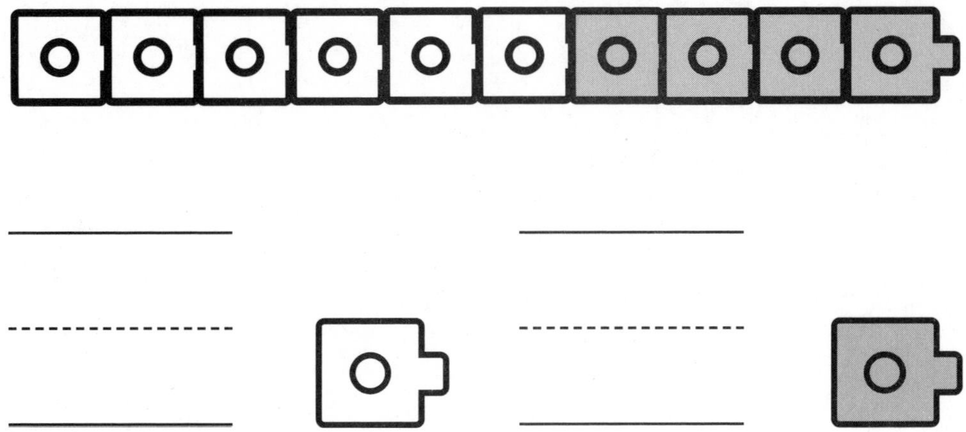

10

11

12

3

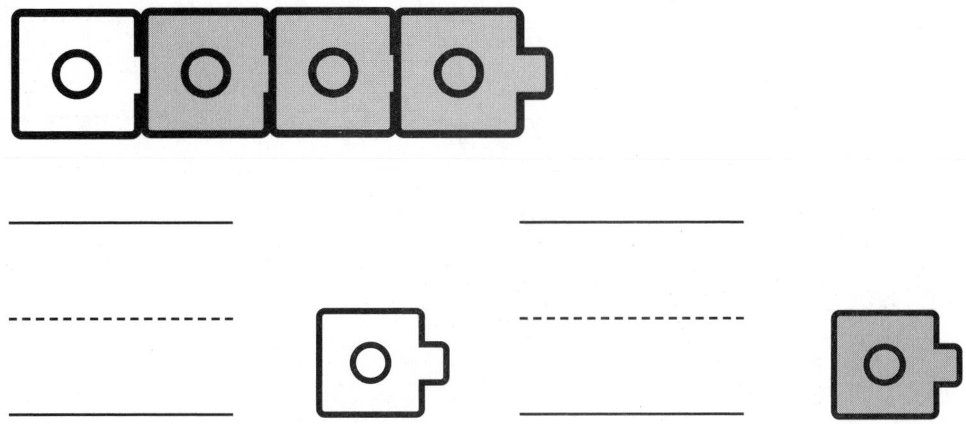

3

4

5

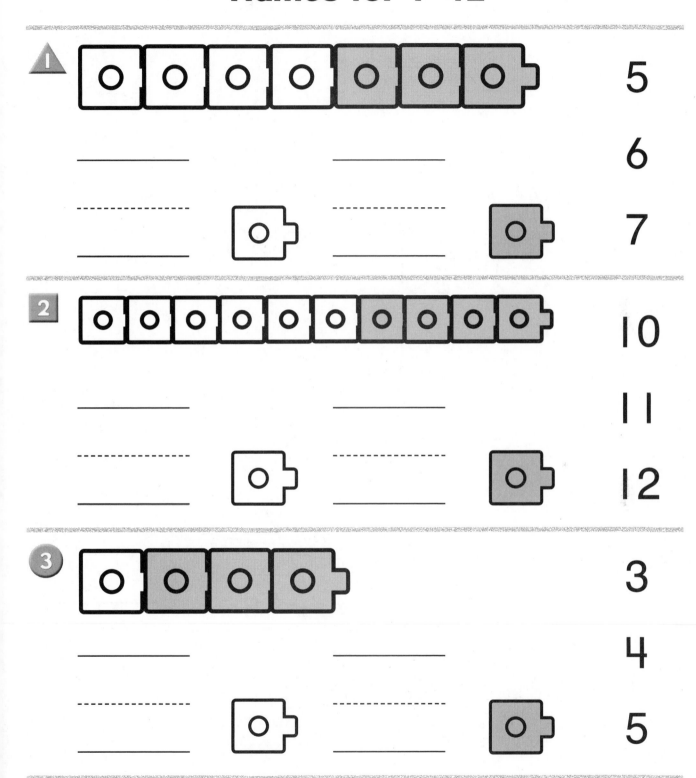

Directions: **1–3** Build the cube train. Count the cubes. Circle the number.
Count the cubes of each color. Write the numbers.

Use with Teacher's Edition pages 145A–146.

Name ______________________________

Order Numbers to 12

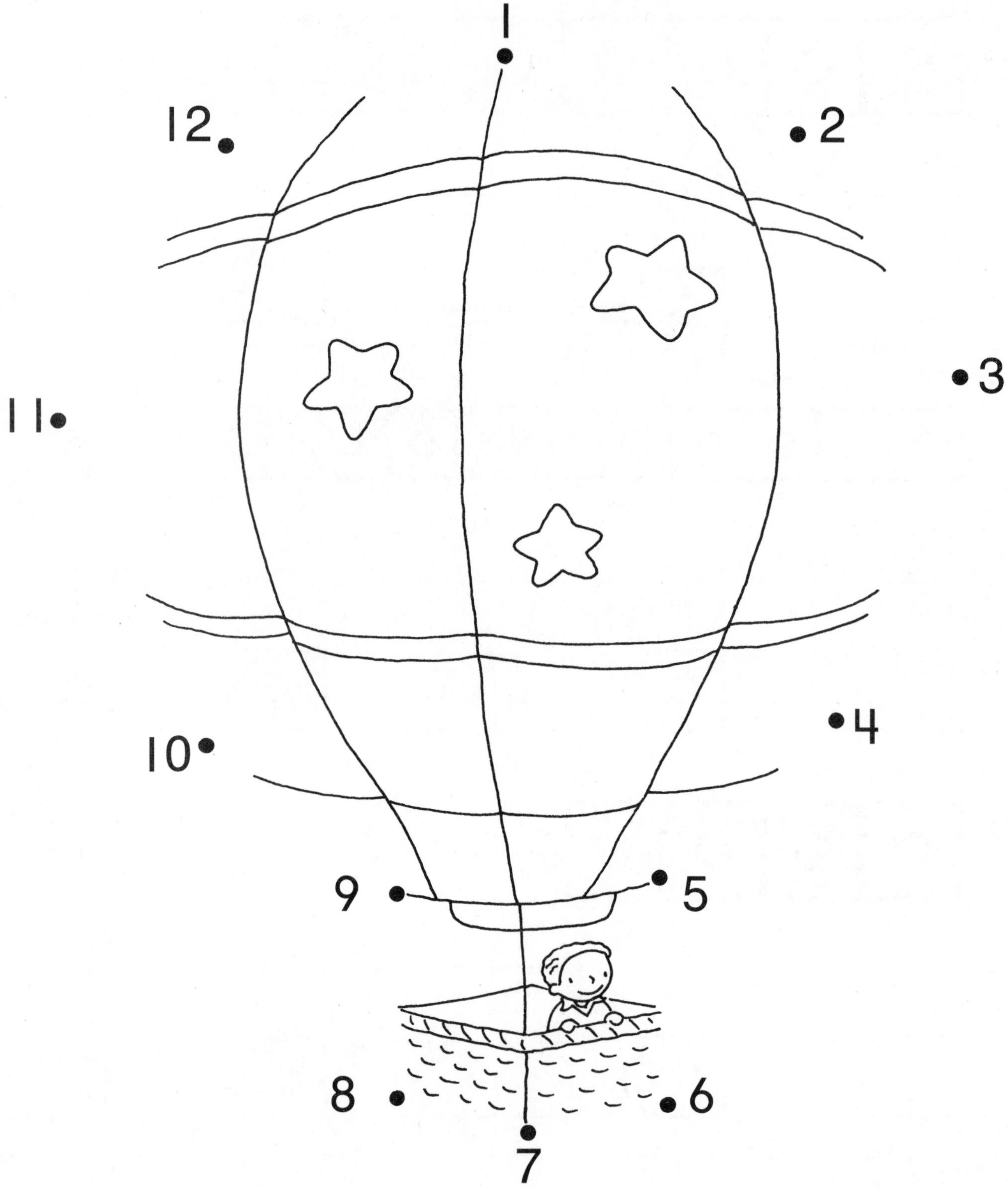

Directions: Connect the dots to make a picture. Color the picture.

Use with Teacher's Edition pages 147A–148.

Name ______________________________

Ordinal Numbers Through 10

Directions: Circle the second child with blue. Circle the tenth child with green. Circle the seventh child with red.

Name ______________________

More and Fewer

1

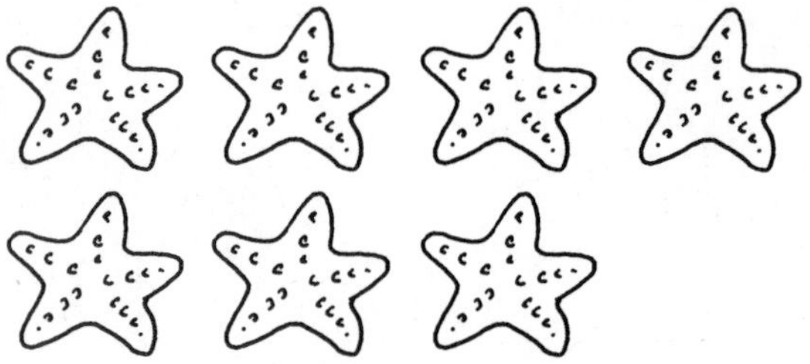

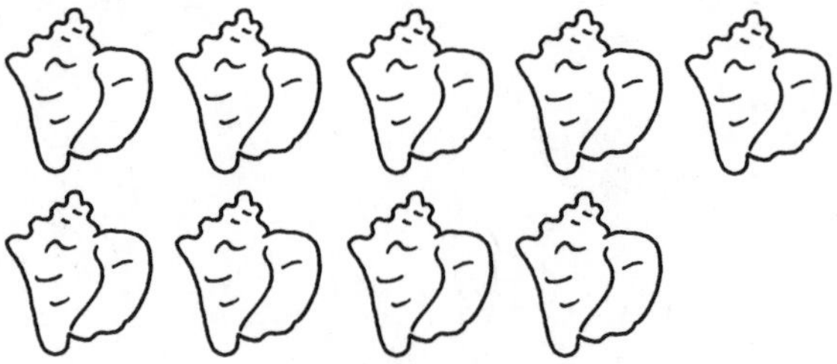

2

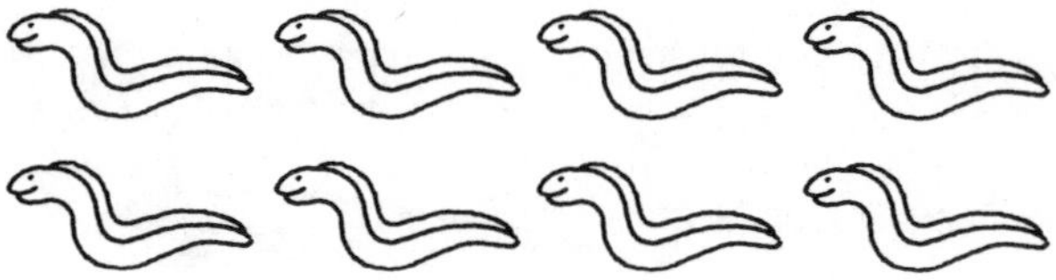

3

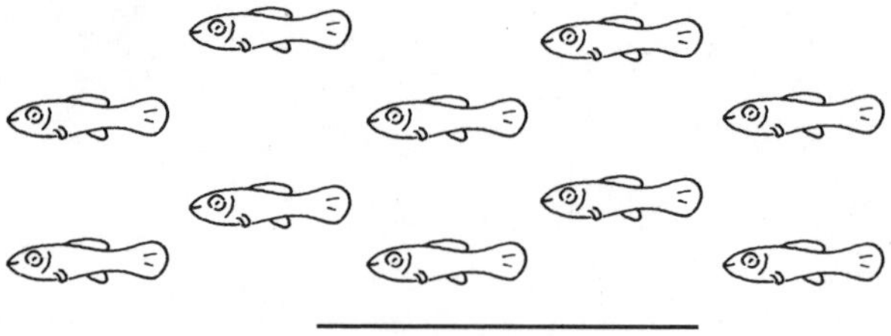

Directions: 1–3 Count. Tell which set has more and which has fewer. Write each number. Circle the greater number.

Use with Teacher's Edition pages 151A–152.

Name ______________________________

Practice 8.5

Estimate Quantities

1

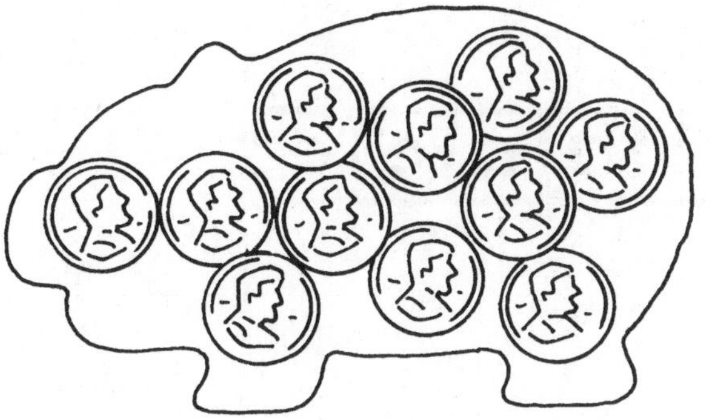

Estimate	Count

2

Estimate	Count

3

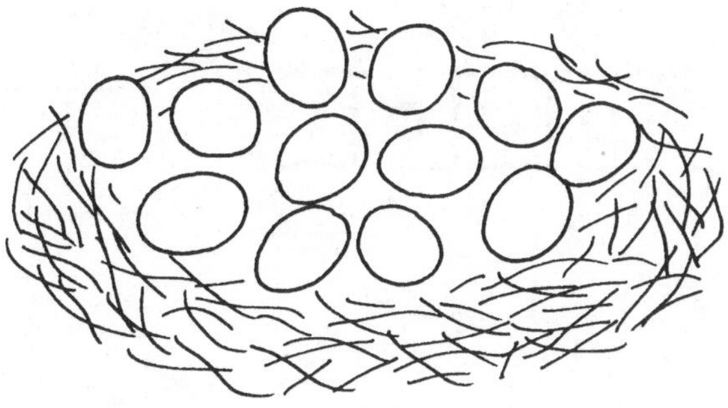

Estimate	Count

4

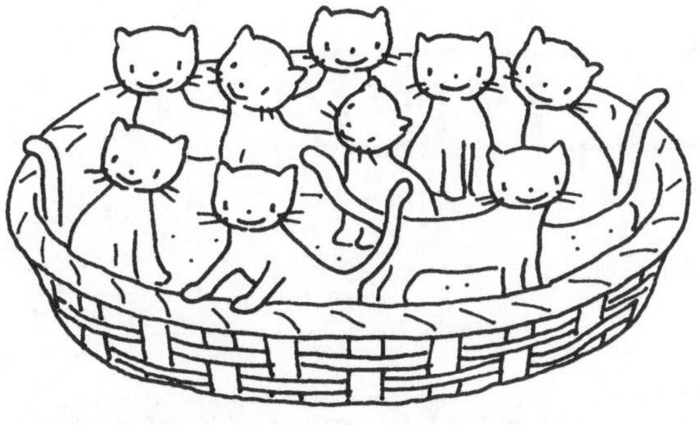

Estimate	Count

Directions: 1–4 Estimate the number in each set. Write the number. Then count the items. Write how many.

Use with Teacher's Edition pages 152A–152D.

Name ________________________

Problem Solving: Act It Out

1

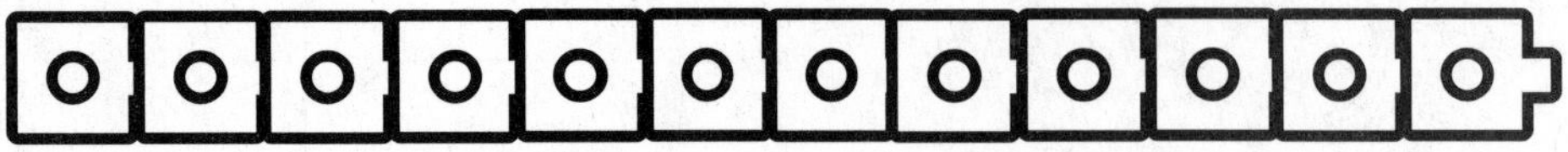

2

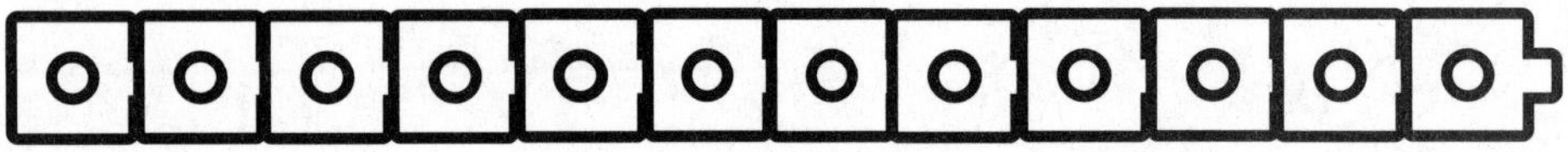

3

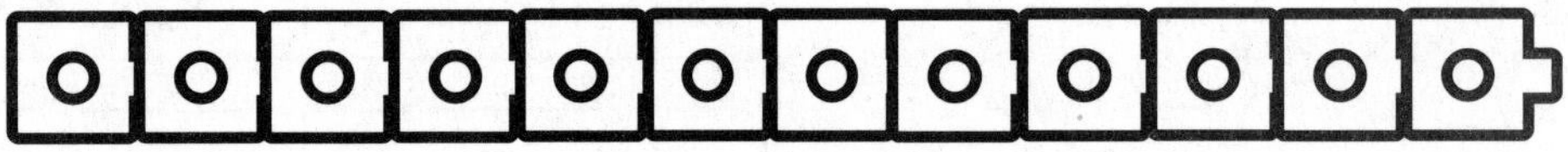

4

Directions: Build the cube train. Break it into equal groups to show: **1** groups of 2 cubes; **2** groups of three cubes; **3** groups of four cubes; **4** groups of six cubes. Draw lines to show where you broke each train. Write the number of equal groups you made.

Use with Teacher's Edition pages 153A–154.

Name ______________________________

Practice 9.1

Times of Day

1

2

3

Directions: Circle the picture that shows: **1** the morning; **2** the afternoon; **3** the evening.

Use with Teacher's Edition pages 165A–166.

Name ______________________________

Practice 9.2

Days and Months on the Calendar

1

Wednesday	Thursday	Friday	Saturday Sunday

2

Saturday	Sunday	Monday	Wednesday Tuesday

3

September	October	November	January December

4

January	February	March	April May

5

May	June	July	September August

Directions: **1–2** Circle the day that comes next. **3–5** Circle the month that comes next.

Use with Teacher's Edition pages 166A–166D.

Name ______________________________

Comparing Temperature

1

2

3

Directions: 1–3 Color a red frame around the picture that shows a hotter day. Color a blue frame around the picture that shows a colder day.

Use with Teacher's Edition pages 167A–168.

Name ____________________

Problem Solving: Use a Picture

May

Sunday	Monday	Tuesday	Wednesday	Thursday	Friday	Saturday
				1	2	3
4	5	6	7	8	9	10
11	12	13	14	15	16	17
18	19	20	21	22	23	24
25	26	27	28	29	30	31

1 ______ Saturdays

2 ______ Thursdays

3 ______ Fridays

4 ______ Wednesdays

Directions: Count and write the number of: **1** Saturdays; **2** Thursdays; **3** Fridays; **4** Wednesdays. Circle the first Tuesday in blue, the last Monday in red, and all the Sundays in green.

Name ______________________________

Practice 9.5

More Time, Less Time

1

2

3

Directions: **1–3** Circle in red the activity that takes more time. Circle in blue the activity that takes less time.

Use with Teacher's Edition pages 171A–172.

Name ________________________________

Order Events

1

2

3

Directions: **1–3** Write the numbers *1, 2,* and *3* to show the order of events from first to last.

Name ______________________________

Time to the Hour

1

_______ o'clock

2

_______ o'clock

3

_______ o'clock

4

_______ o'clock

5

_______ o'clock

Directions: 1–5 Write the time shown on the clock.

Use with Teacher's Edition pages 175A–176.

Name ____________________

More Time to the Hour

1. 3:00

____________ o'clock

2. 9:00

____________ o'clock

3. 5:00

____________ o'clock

4. 12:00

____________ o'clock

5. 2:00

____________ o'clock

Directions: **1–5** Write the time shown on the clock.

Name ______________________________

Compare Digital and Analog Clocks

1

2

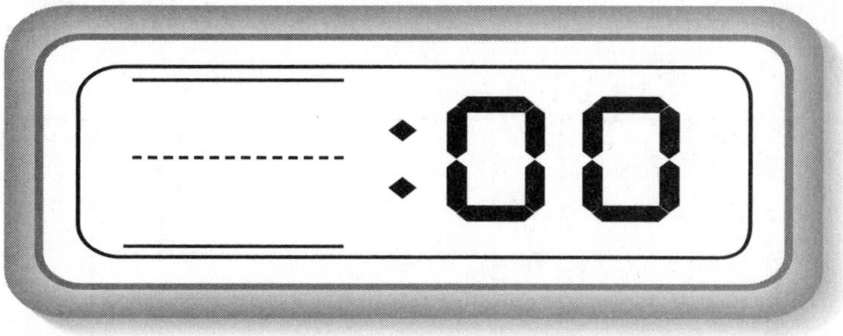

3

4

5

Directions: 1–5 Write the time shown on the clock.

Use with Teacher's Edition pages 179A–180.

Name ______________________________

Sort and Graph Coins

Directions: Count each kind of coin at the top of the page. Color the boxes to show how many.

Use with Teacher's Edition pages 184A–184D.

Name ______________________________________

Penny

1

2

3

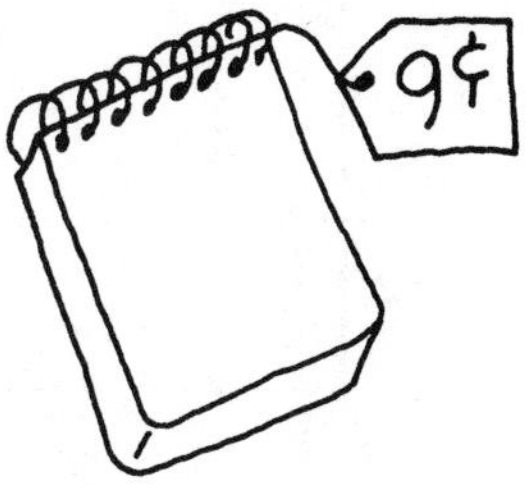

4

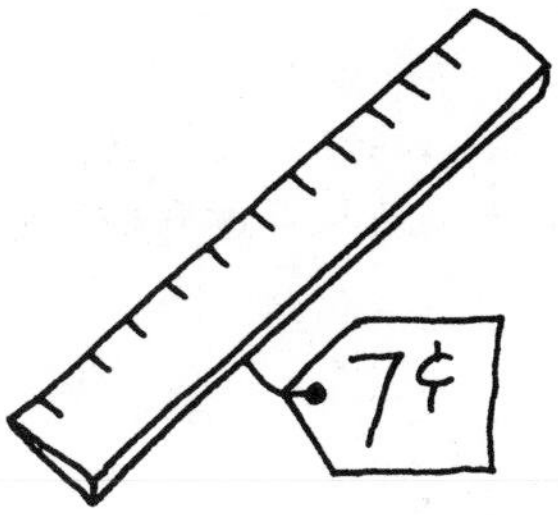

5

Directions: 1–5 Use pennies to show each price. Draw the pennies.

Name ______________________________

Nickel

1

6¢ 8¢ 10¢

2

6¢ 7¢ 8¢

3

8¢ 7¢ 6¢

4

10¢ 11¢ 12¢

Directions: 1–4 Circle the price tag that matches the number of cents.

Name ______________________

Dime

1

10¢ 5¢ 1¢

2

9¢ 10¢ 11¢

3

9¢ 10¢ 11¢

4

12¢ 11¢ 10¢

5

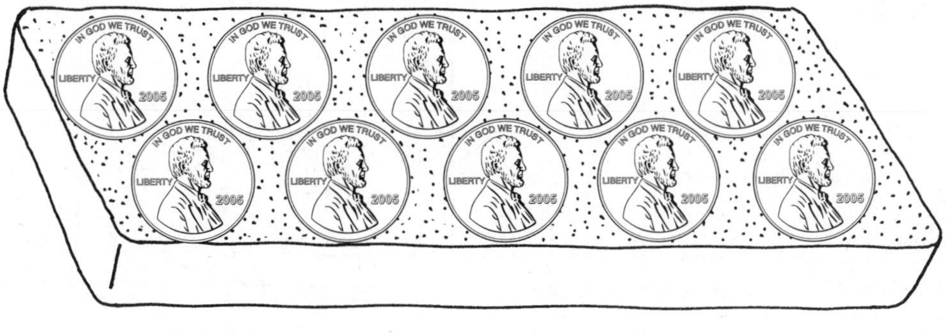

9¢ 10¢ 11¢

Directions: 1–5 Circle the number of cents.

Use with Teacher's Edition pages 189A–190.

Name ____________________

Quarter

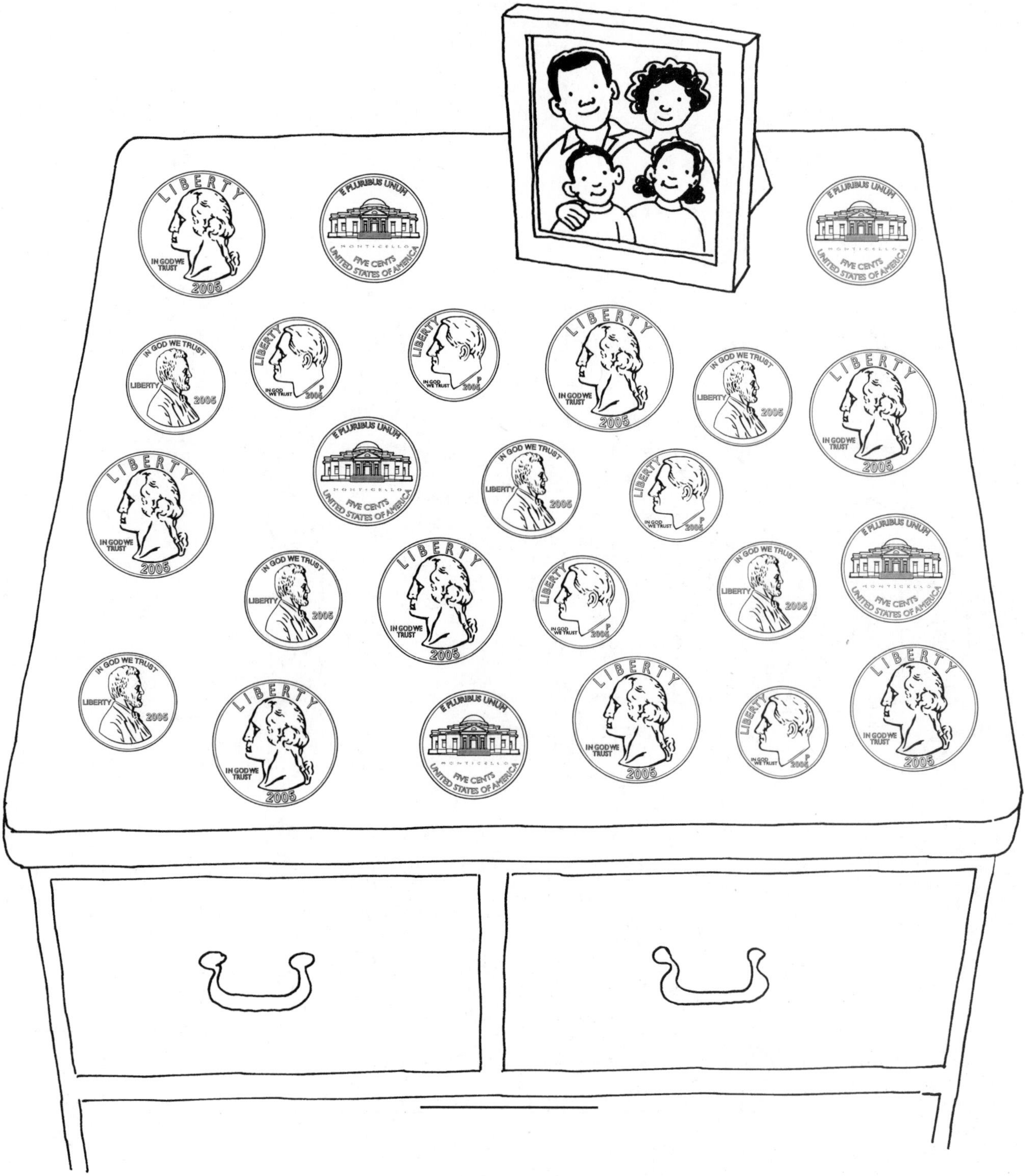

______

Directions: Circle all the quarters. Count and write the number of quarters.

Use with Teacher's Edition pages 191A–192.

Name ________________________

Problem Solving: Act It Out

______ ¢

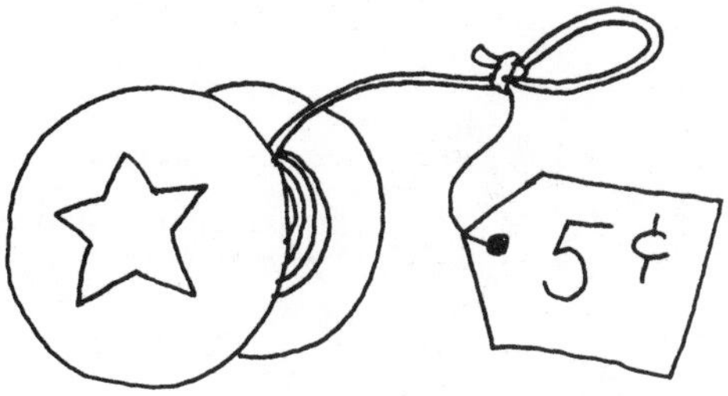

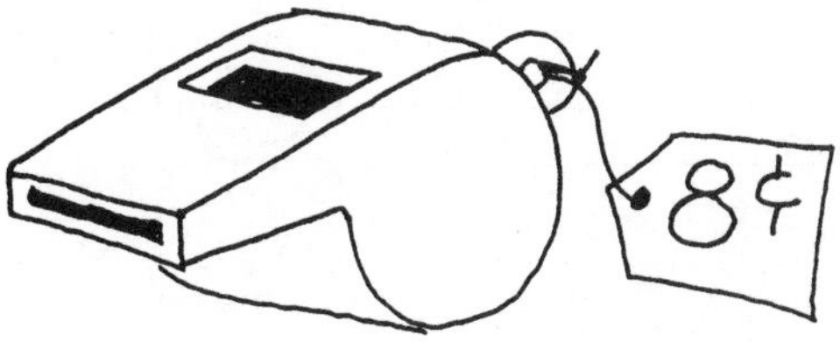

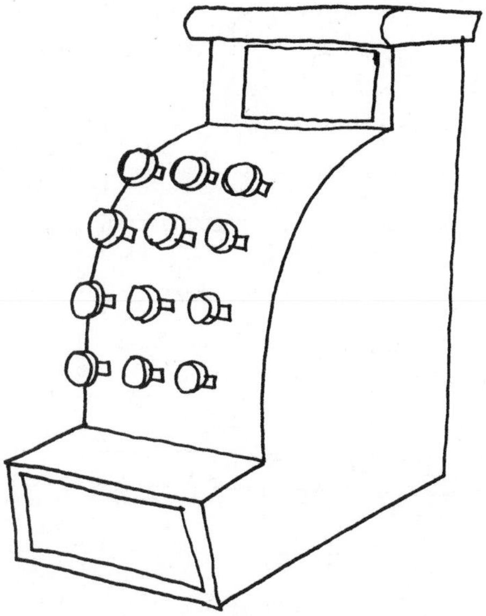

______ ¢

Directions: Place 10 pennies on the purse. Circle an item you want to buy. Move that many cents to the cash register. Write how much you spent. Write what you have left in the purse.

Use with Teacher's Edition pages 193A–194.

Name ____________________

Compare Length

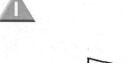

1

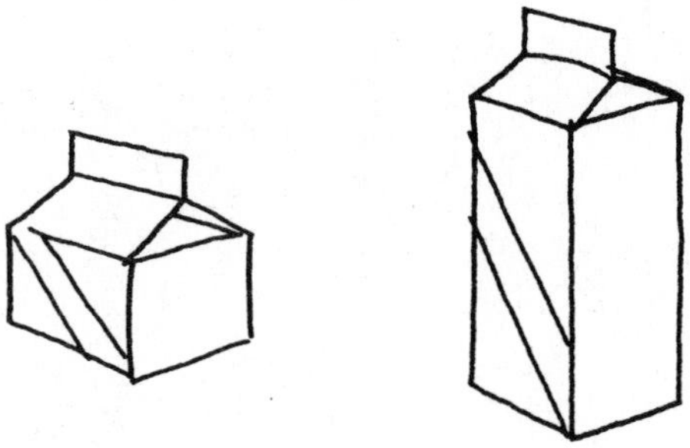

2

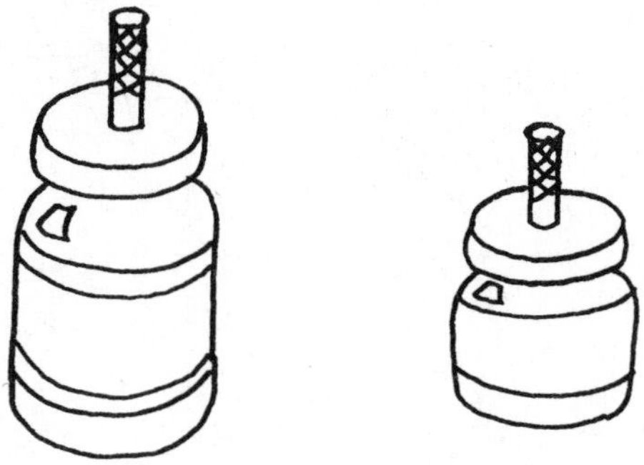

3

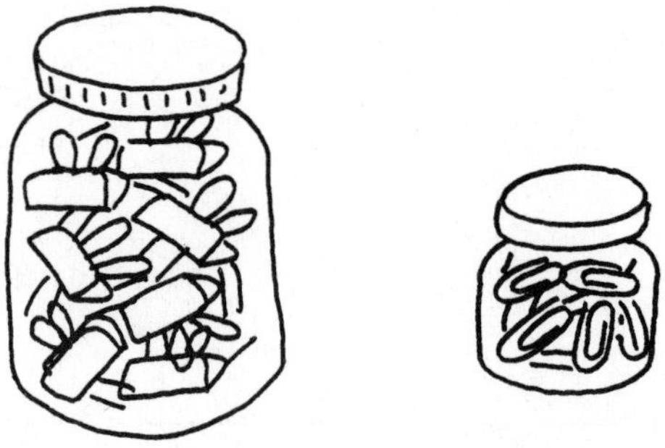

4

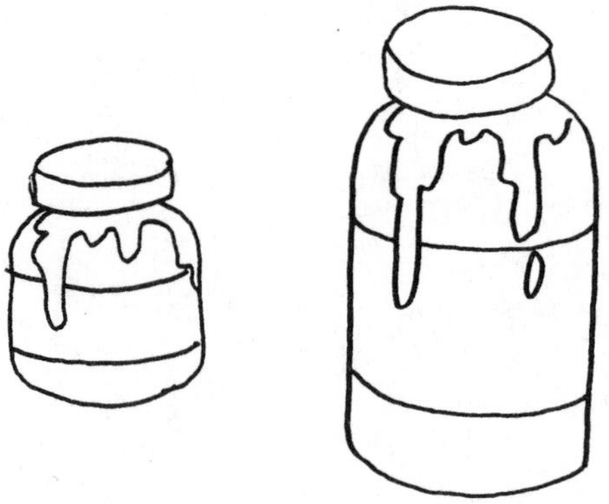

5

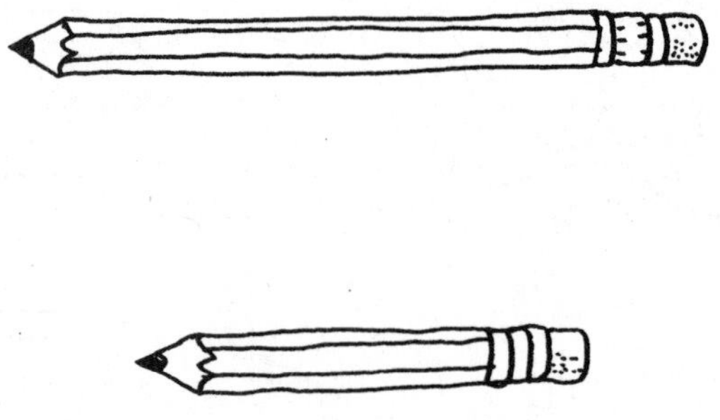

6

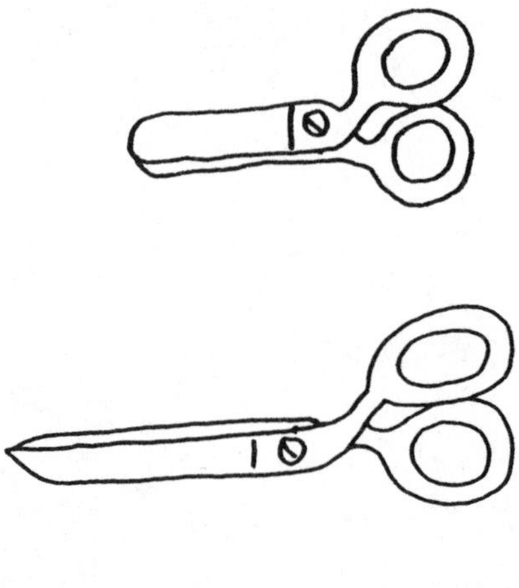

Directions: **1–4** Circle the taller one. Underline the shorter one. **5–6** Circle the longer one. Underline the shorter one.

Use with Teacher's Edition pages 205A–206.

Name ______________________________

Order by Length

1

2

3

4

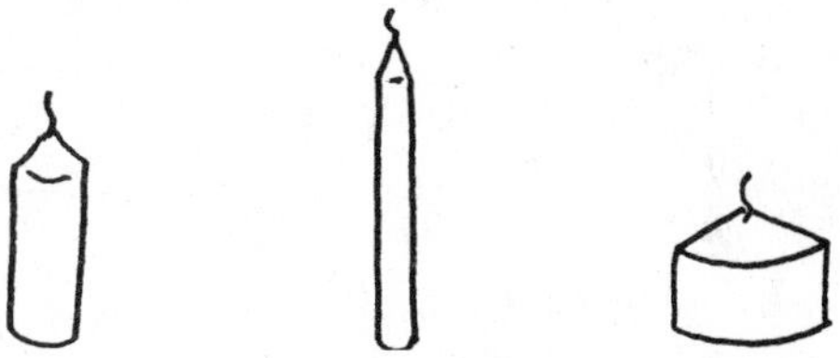

5

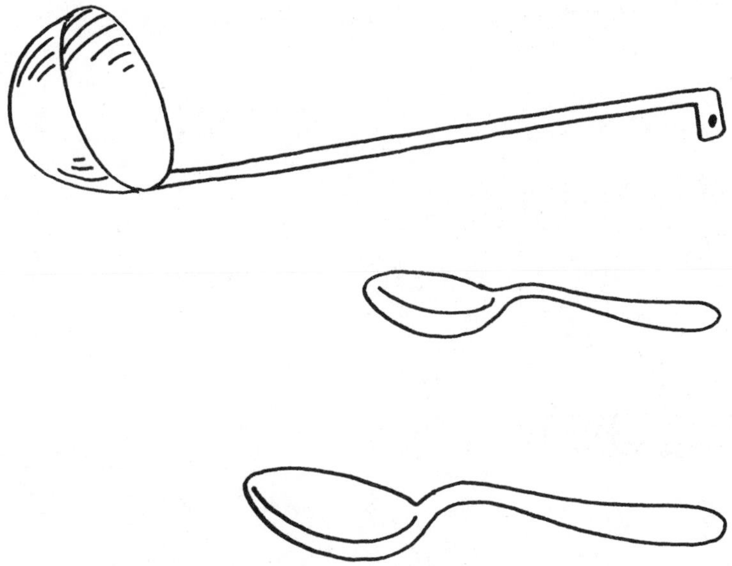

Directions: **1–4** Write the numbers *1*, *2*, and *3* to order the items from shortest to tallest.
5 Write the numbers *1*, *2*, and *3* to order the items from shortest to longest.

Use with Teacher's Edition pages 207A–208.

Name ____________________

Practice 11.3

Measure Length

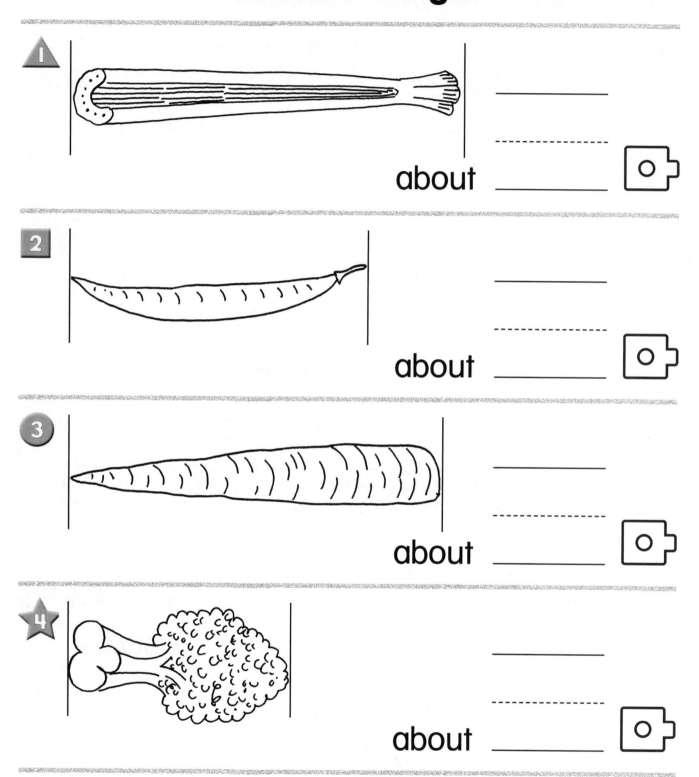

1

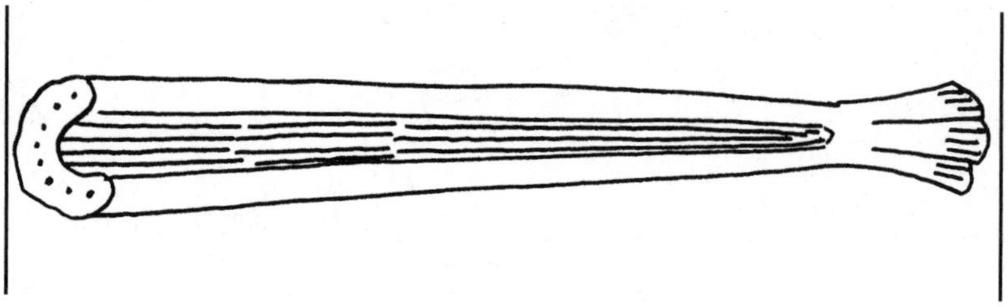

about ______

2

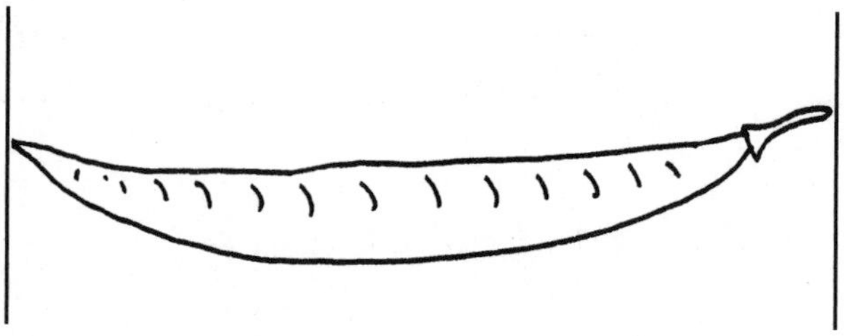

about ______

3

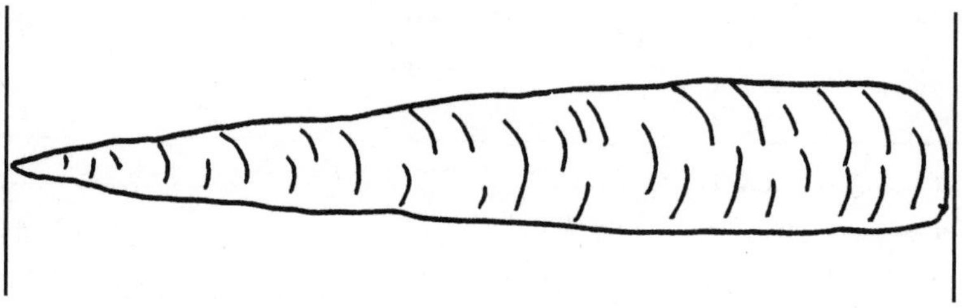

about ______

4

about ______

Directions: 1–4 Use cubes to measure the length. Record the length.

Use with Teacher's Edition pages 209A–210.

Name ____________________

Practice 11.4

Estimate and Measure Length

1

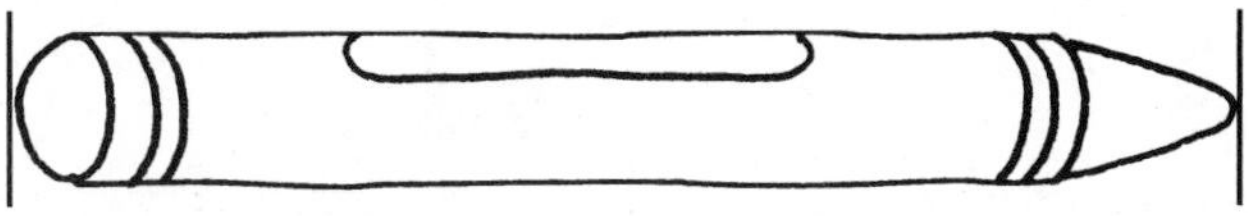

Estimate ______ Measure ______

about ______ about ______

2

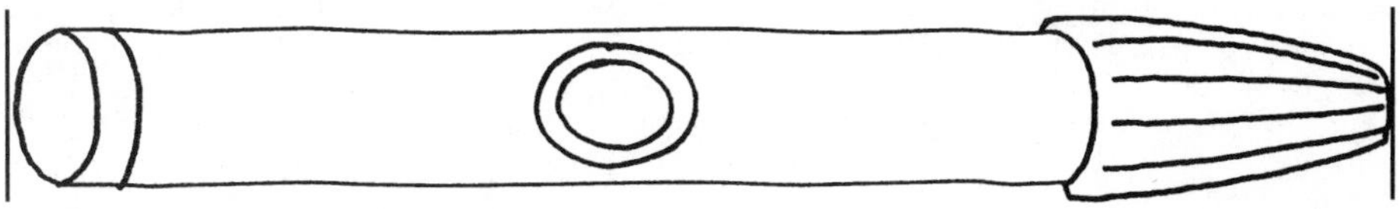

Estimate ______ Measure ______

about ______ about ______

3

Estimate ______ Measure ______

about ______ about ______

Directions: 1–3 Estimate how many cubes long. Measure. Record the length. Compare the measurement to the estimate.

Use with Teacher's Edition pages 211A–212.

Name ______________________

Explore Area

1

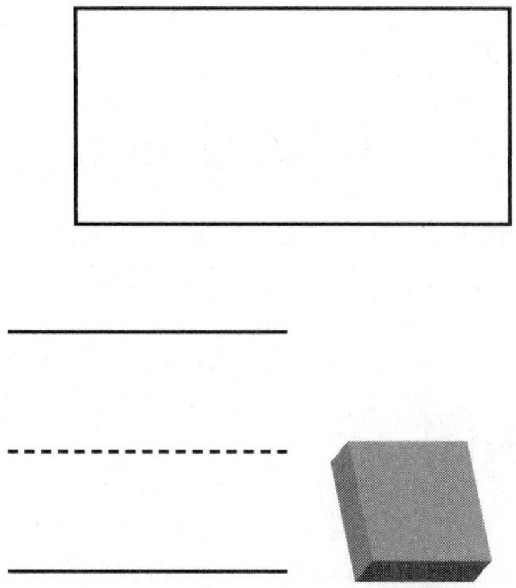

2

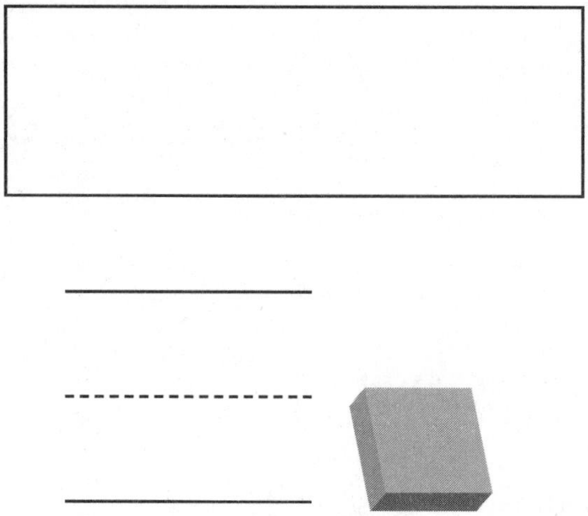

3

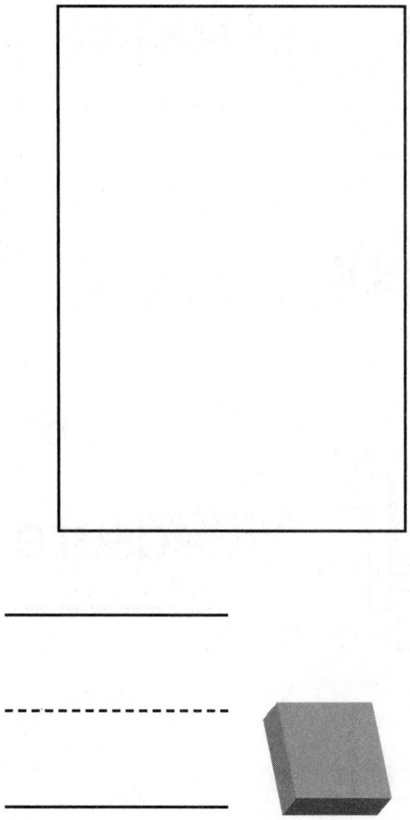

4

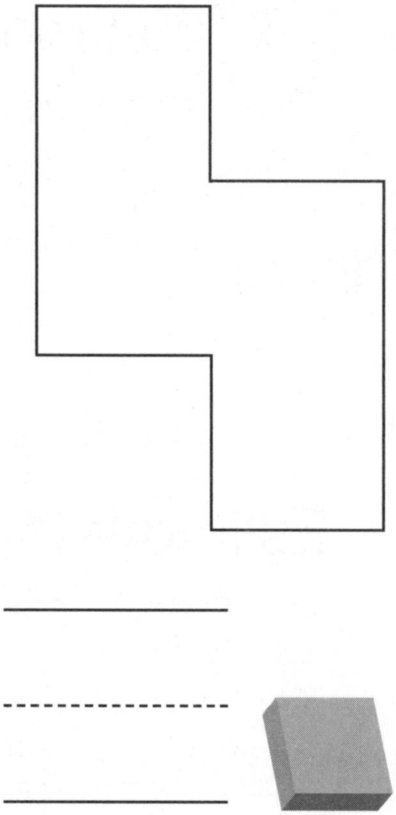

Directions: **1–4** Use square pattern blocks to find the area.

Use with Teacher's Edition pages 212A–212D.

Name ______________________

Practice 11.6

Problem Solving: Act It Out

1

Estimate

______

about ______ 

Measure

______

about ______ 

2

Estimate

______

about ______ 

Measure

______

about ______ 

3

Estimate

______

about ______ 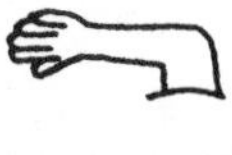

Measure

______

about ______ 

Directions: Estimate the number of: **1** hands tall the chair is; **2** foot lengths long the rug is; **3** forearms the bookshelf is. Measure and record. Compare measurements to estimates.

Use with Teacher's Edition pages 213A–214.

Name ____________________

Practice 12.1

Compare Weight

1

2

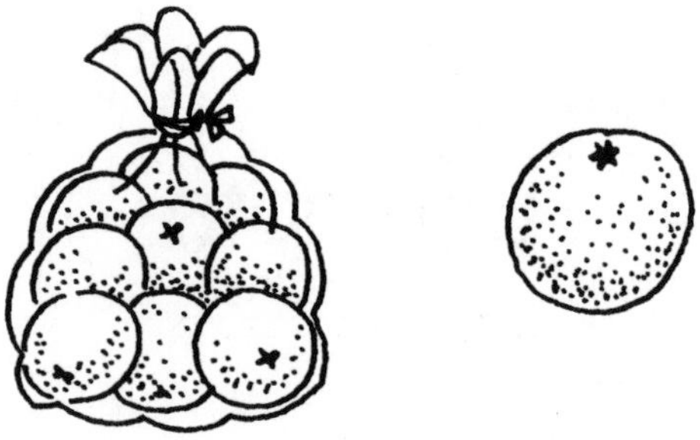

3

4

5

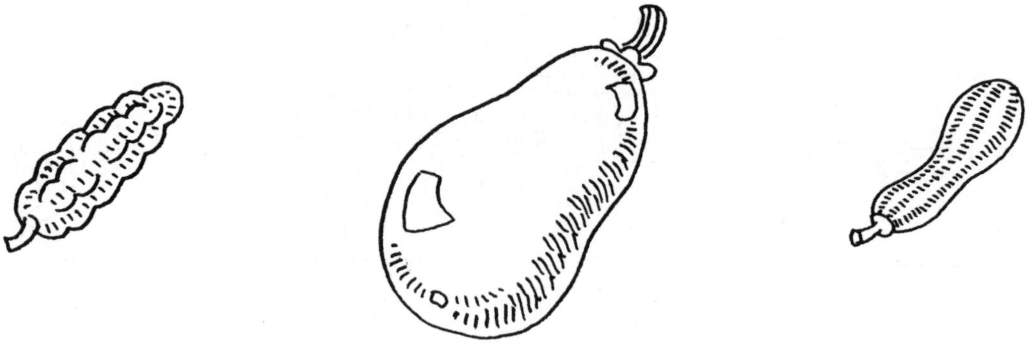

Directions: 1–4 Circle the heavier one. Underline the lighter one. **5** Circle the two that are about the same weight.

Use with Teacher's Edition pages 219A–220.

Name ______________________

Order by Weight

1

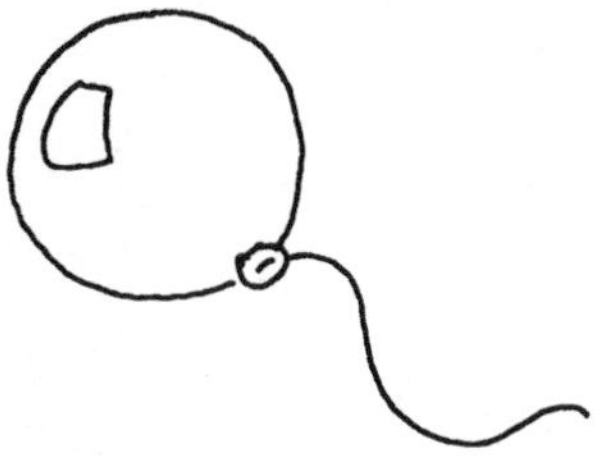

2

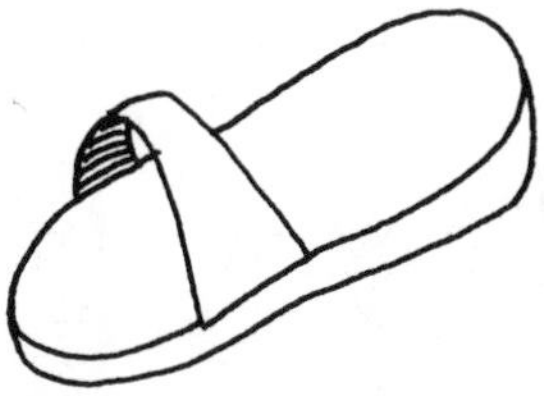

3

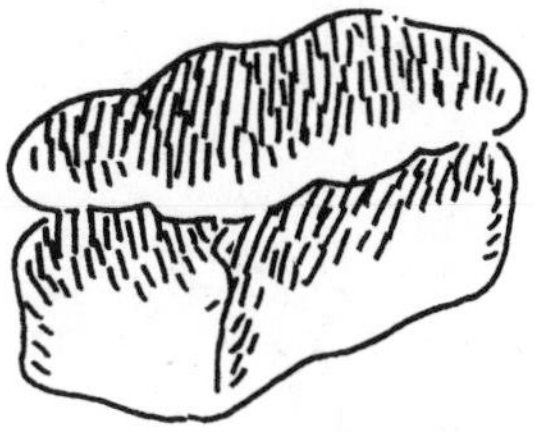
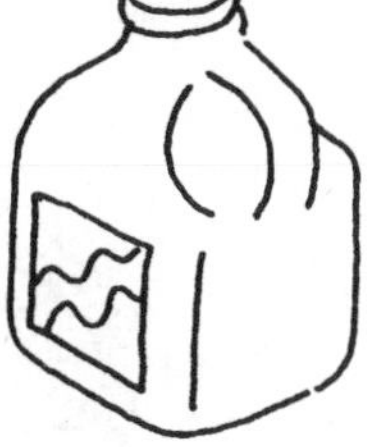

Directions: 1–3 Write the numbers *1, 2,* and *3* to order the items from lightest to heaviest.

Use with Teacher's Edition pages 221A–222.

Name ______________________________

Measure Weight

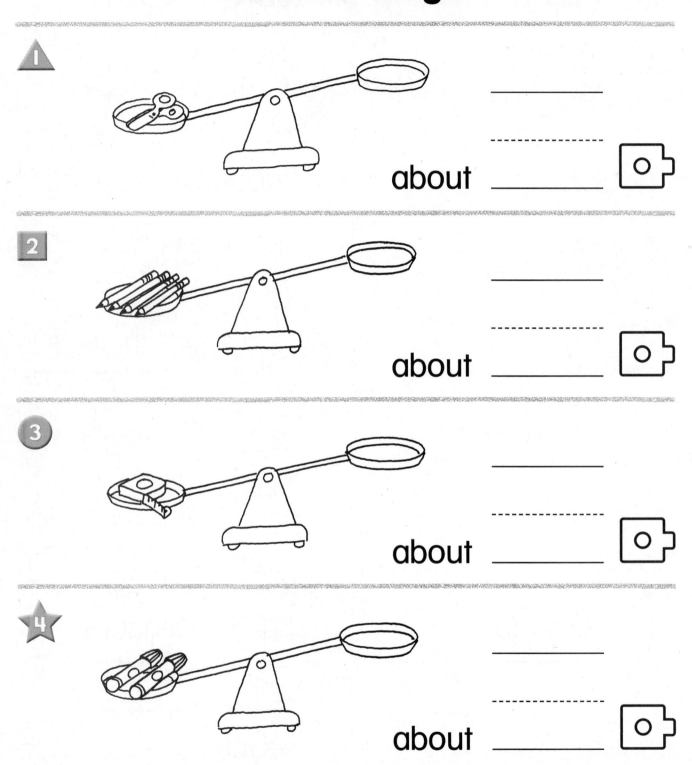

1

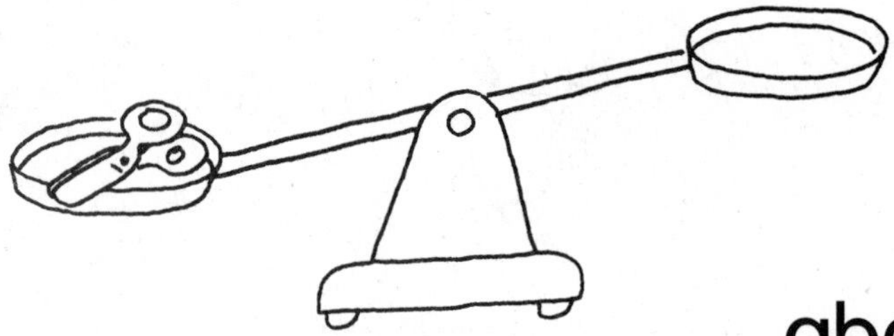

______

- - - - - - - - -

about ______ 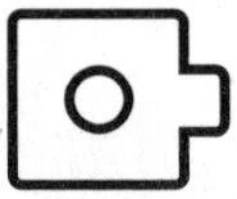

2

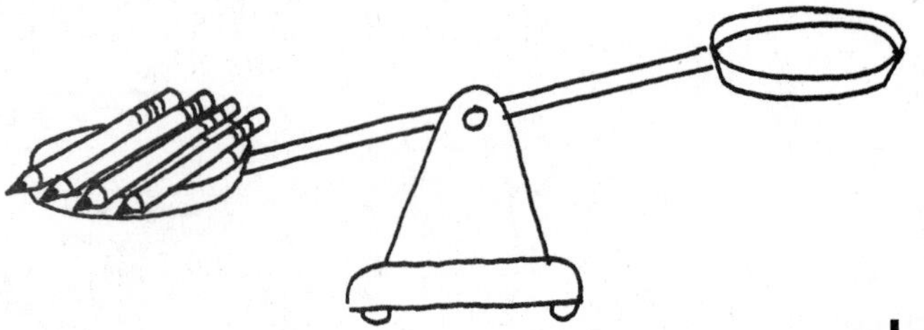

______

- - - - - - - - -

about ______ 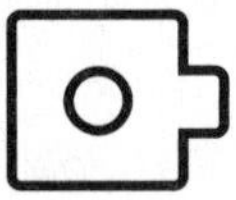

3

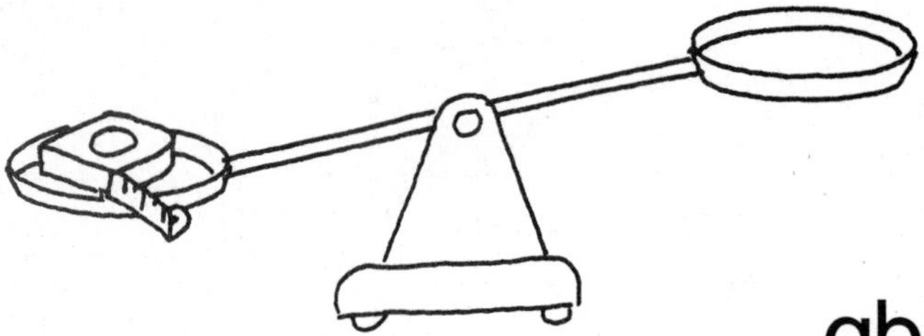

______

- - - - - - - - -

about ______ 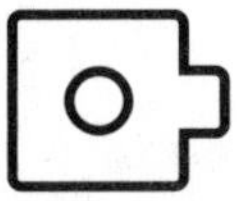

4

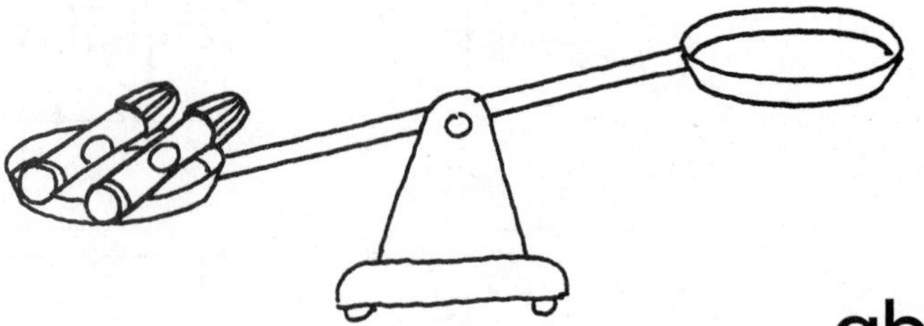

______

- - - - - - - - -

about ______ 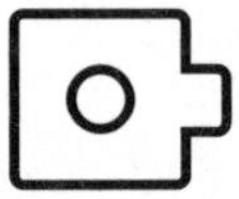

Directions: 1–4 Use objects like the ones shown. Use cubes to balance the buckets. Record the number of cubes.

Use with Teacher's Edition pages 222A–222D.

Name ________________________

Practice 12.4

Estimate and Measure Weight

1

Estimate ________

Measure ________

about ________ (cube)   about ________ (cube)

2

Estimate ________

Measure ________

about ________ (cube)   about ________ (cube)

3

Estimate ________

Measure ________

about ________ (cube)   about ________ (cube)

4

Estimate ________

Measure ________

about ________ (cube)   about ________ (cube)

Directions: 1–4 Use objects like the ones shown. Estimate how many cubes are needed to balance the buckets. Measure. Record the number of cubes. Compare the measurement to the estimate.

Use with Teacher's Edition pages 223A–224.

Name ____________________

Compare Capacity

1

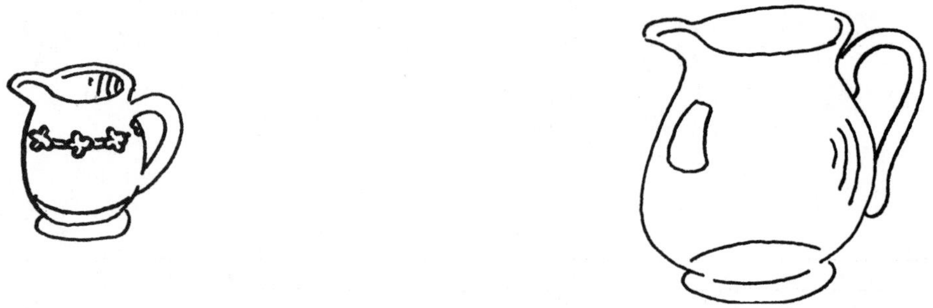

2

3

4

Directions: 1–4 Compare the kinds of containers. Circle the one that holds more. Underline the one that holds less.

Use with Teacher's Edition pages 225A–226.

Name ______________________________

Order by Capacity

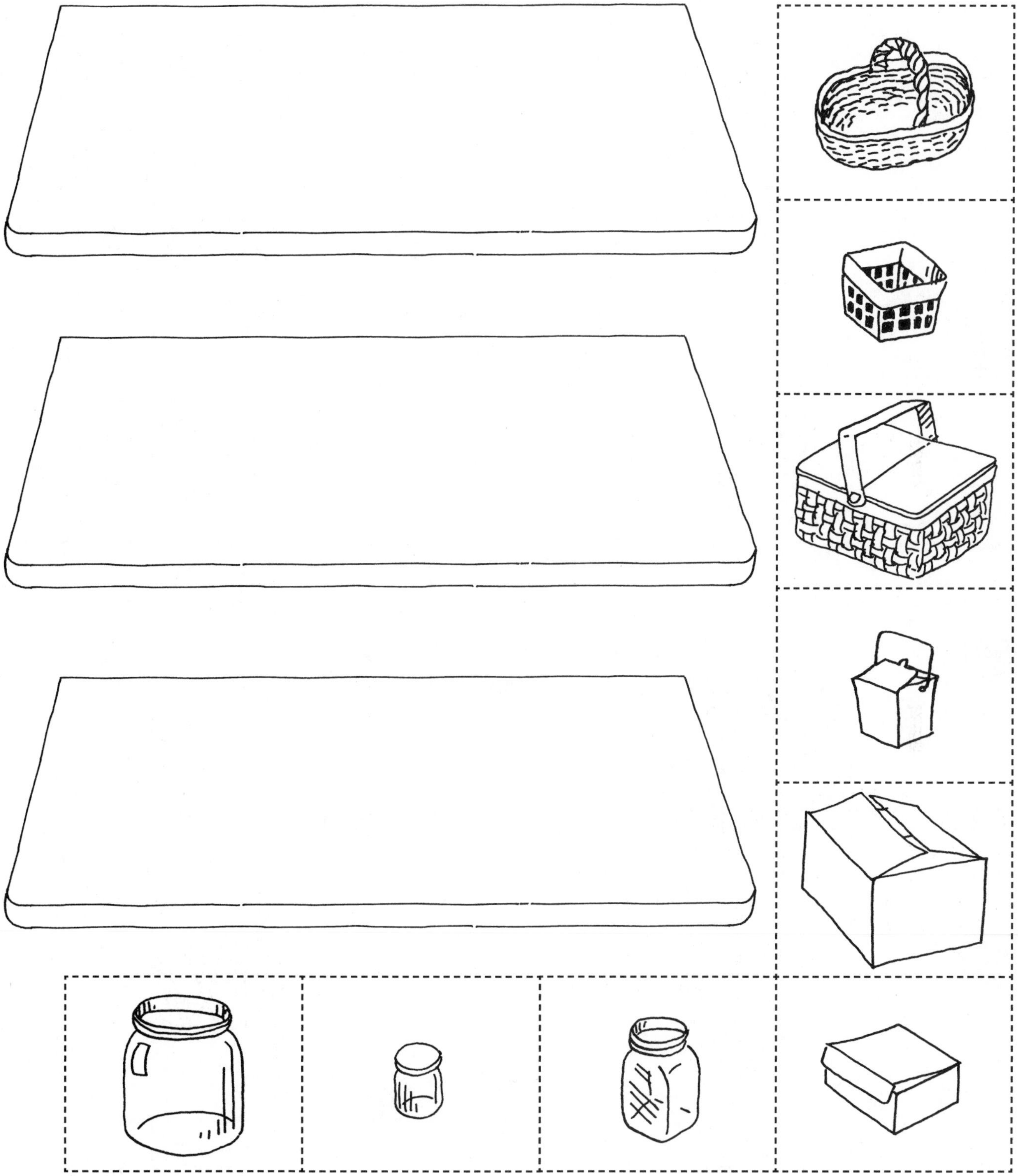

Directions: Cut out the pictures. Sort them by kind. Glue them on the shelves in order from the one that holds the least to the one that holds the most.

Use with Teacher's Edition pages 227A–228.

Name ______________________________

Measure Capacity

1

about ________ 

2

about ________ 

3

about ________ 

4

about ________ 

Directions: 1–4 Use a container like the one shown. Measure to find out how many cups of beans are needed to fill the container. Record the number of cups.

Name ______________________________

Practice 12.8

Estimate and Measure Capacity

1

Estimate

about ________ 

Measure

about ________ 

2

Estimate

about ________ 

Measure

about ________ 

3

Estimate

about ________ 

Measure

about ________ 

4

Estimate

about ________ 

Measure

about ________ 

Directions: 1–4 Use a container like the one shown. Estimate how many cups of beans are needed to fill the container. Measure. Record the number of cups. Compare the measurement to the estimate.

Use with Teacher's Edition pages 229A–230.

Name ___________________________

Tools for Measuring

1

2

3

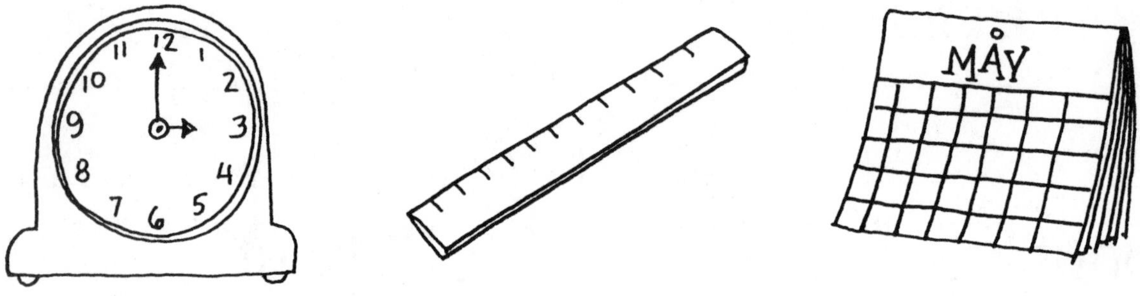

4

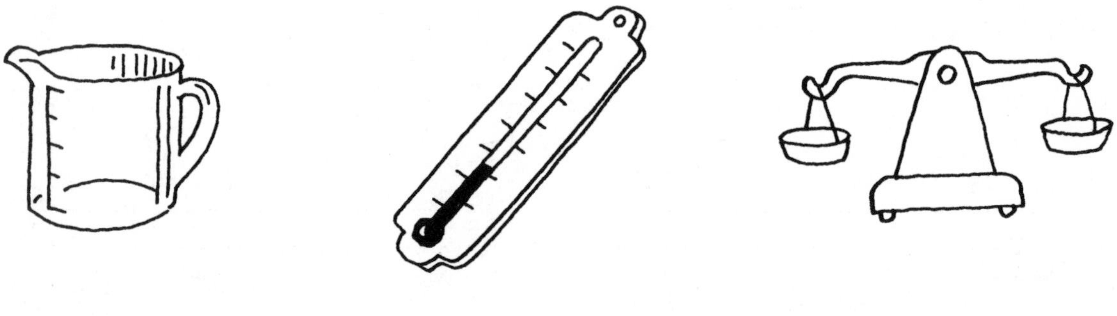

Directions: Circle the tool used to: **1** tell if it is time to go to bed; **2** measure how long a box is; **3** count how many days are left in the month; **4** find out if a pencil and a crayon weigh about the same.

Name ____________________

Practice 12.10

Problem Solving: Use Logical Reasoning

1

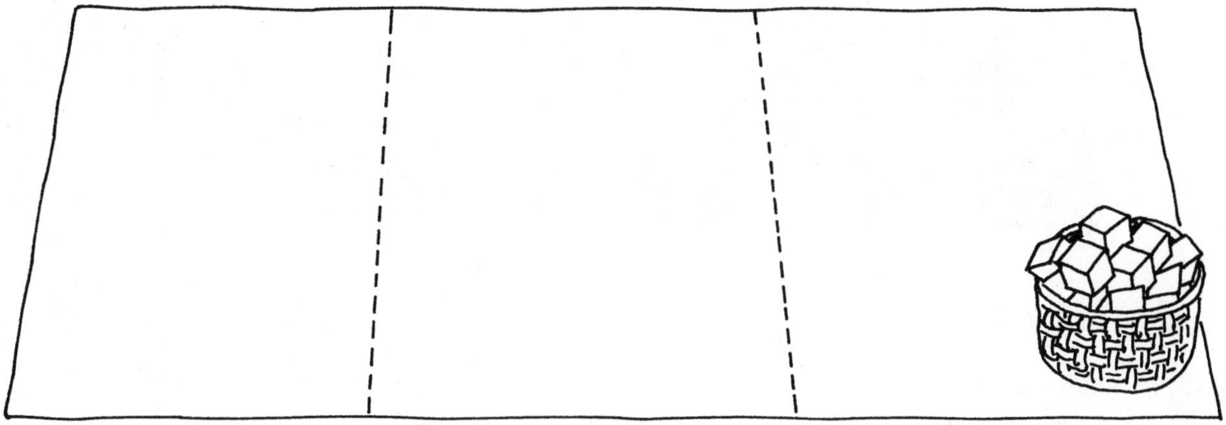

2

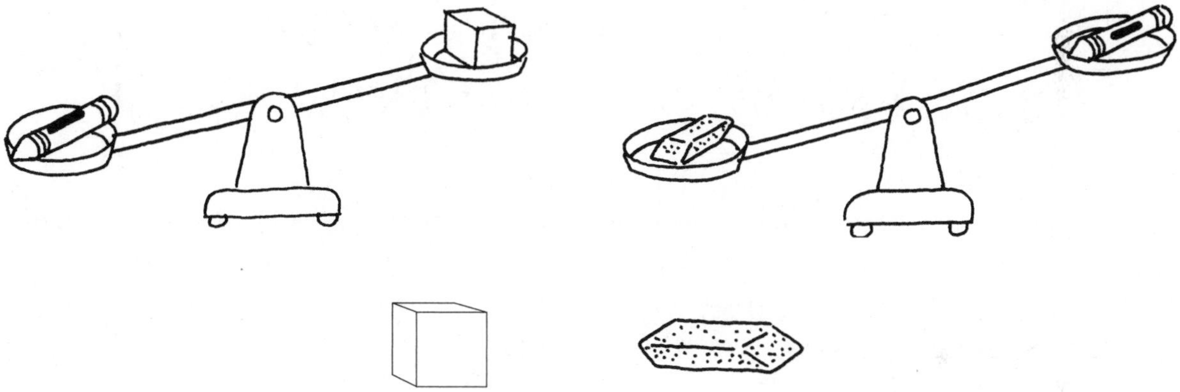

3

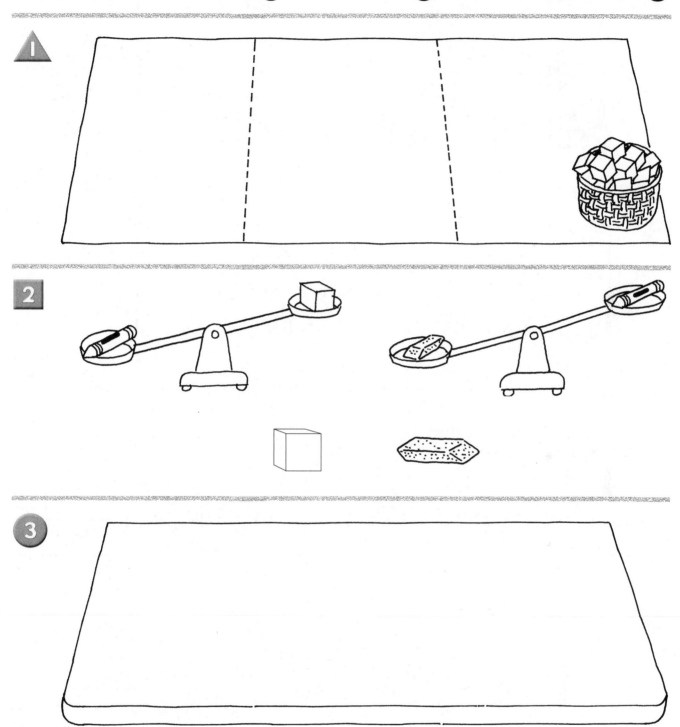

Directions: **1** Draw three block towers. The middle tower is taller than the first tower. The first tower is taller than the last. Circle the tallest tower. **2** Circle the item that is lighter. **3** Draw a blue cup that holds less than a green cup. Draw a red cup that holds less than the blue cup. Circle the cup that holds the most.

Use with Teacher's Edition pages 233A–234.

Name ____________________

Practice 13.1

Model Addition

1

____
____
____

2

____
____
____

3

____
____
____

4

____
____
____

Directions: 1–4 Tell a joining story about the picture. Use counters to model the story. Count. Write how many in all.

Use with Teacher's Edition pages 244A–244D.

Name ______________________

Practice 13.2

Add 1 to Numbers 0–9

1

______
______
______

2

______
______
______

3

______
______
______

4

______
______
______

Directions: 1–4 Tell a story about how the picture shows adding one. Write how many in all.

Use with Teacher's Edition pages 245A–246.

Name ______________________________

Add 2 to Numbers 0–5

1

3 + 2 = ____

2

4 + 2 = ____

3

5 + 2 = ____

Directions: 1–3 Show each number with counters. Draw. Write how many in all.

Use with Teacher's Edition pages 247A–248.

Name ____________________

Add 2 to Numbers 6–8

1

____ + ____ = ____

2

____ + ____ = ____

3

____ + ____ = ____

Directions: 1–3 Write the number in each group. Add. Write the sum.

Use with Teacher's Edition pages 249A–250.

Name ____________________

Add Pennies

1

_____ _____ _____

_____ ¢ + _____ ¢ = _____ ¢

2

_____ _____ _____

_____ ¢ + _____ ¢ = _____ ¢

3

_____ _____ _____

_____ ¢ + _____ ¢ = _____ ¢

Directions: 1–3 Write the number in each group. Add. Write the sum.

Use with Teacher's Edition pages 251A–252.

Name ______________________

Practice Addition

1

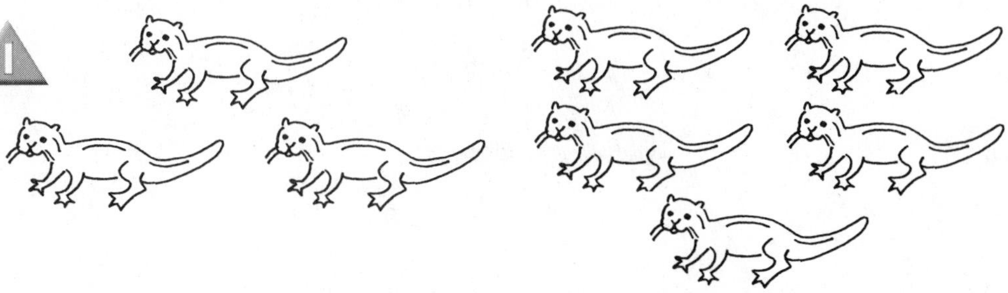

____ + ____ = ____

2

____ + ____ = ____

3

____ + ____ = ____

Directions: 1–3 Write the number in each group. Add. Write the sum.

Use with Teacher's Edition pages 253A–254.

Name ________________________

Doubles

1

_____ + _____ = _____

2

_____ + _____ = _____

3

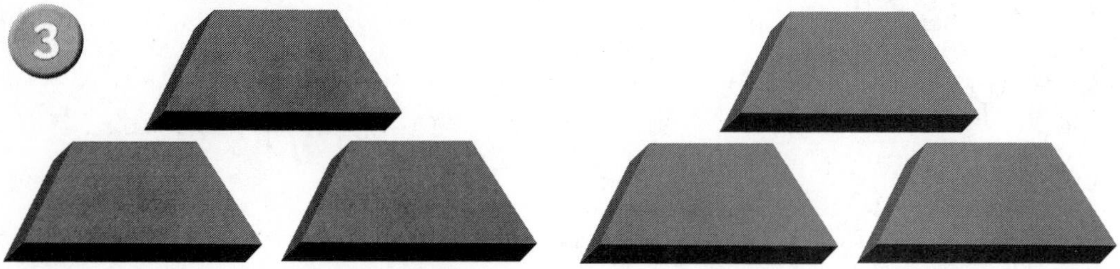

_____ + _____ = _____

Directions: 1–3 Write the number in each group. Add. Write the sum.

Name ________________

Problem Solving: Draw a Picture

1

$3 + 7 =$ ____

2

$3 + 5 =$ ____

Directions: 1–2 Draw a picture to match the fact. Add. Write the sum.

Name ________________________

Model Subtraction

1

____
- - - - - - - -
____

2

____
- - - - - - - -
____

3

____
- - - - - - - -
____

4

____
- - - - - - - -
____

Directions: 1–4 Count how many in all. Use a sticky note to cover the ones that are leaving. Write how many are left.

Use with Teacher's Edition pages 262A–262D.

Name ______________________

Practice 14.2

Subtract 1 From Numbers 0–9

1

2

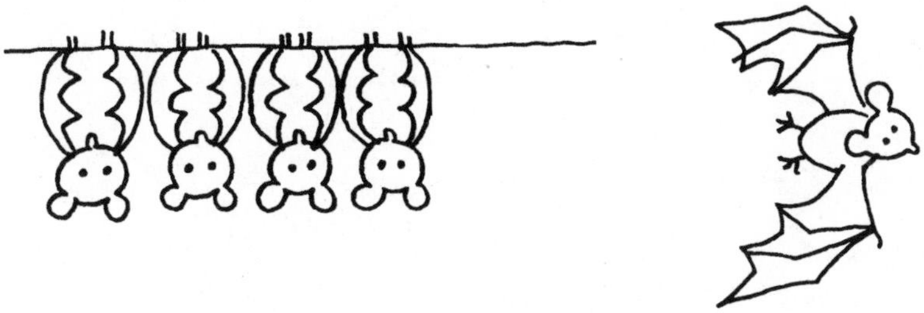

3

4

Directions: 1–4 Count how many in all. Circle and cross out the one that is leaving. Write how many are left.

Use with Teacher's Edition pages 263A–264.

Name ______________________

Subtract 2 From Numbers 2–5

1

$4 - 2 =$ ____

2

$5 - 2 =$ ____

3

$3 - 2 =$ ____

Directions: **1–3** Show the first number with counters. Draw the counters. Circle and cross out the group of 2. Write how many are left.

Use with Teacher's Edition pages 265A–266.

Name ____________________

Subtract 2 From Numbers 6–10

1

____ − ____ = ____

2

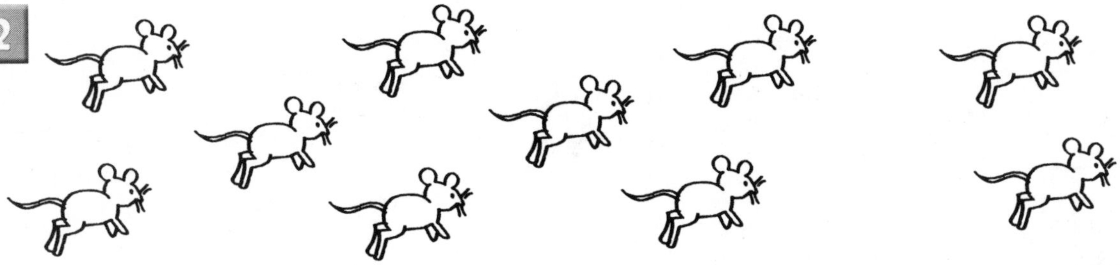

____ − ____ = ____

3

____ − ____ = ____

Directions: 1–3 Write the number of animals in all. Use counters to model taking away two. Circle and cross out two. Write the number you crossed out. Write the difference.

Use with Teacher's Edition pages 267A–268.

Name ______________________

Subtract Pennies

1

______ ¢ − 3 ¢ = ______ ¢

2

______ ¢ − 1 ¢ = ______ ¢

3

______ ¢ − 2 ¢ = ______ ¢

4

______ ¢ − 3 ¢ = ______ ¢

Directions: 1–4 Count and write the number of pennies in all. Circle and cross out the number shown. Write how many are left.

Use with Teacher's Edition pages 269A–270.

Name ____________________

Practice 14.6

Practice Subtraction

1

______ − ______ = ______

2

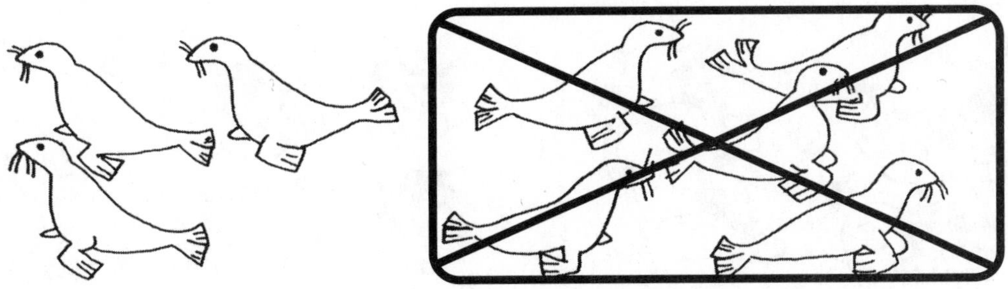

______ − ______ = ______

3

______ − ______ = ______

Directions: 1–3 Write a subtraction sentence to match the picture.

Use with Teacher's Edition pages 271A–272.

Name ______________________

Practice 14.7

Relate Addition and Subtraction

1

___ + ___ = ___

___ − ___ = ___

2

___ + ___ = ___

___ − ___ = ___

3

___ + ___ = ___

___ − ___ = ___

Directions: 1–3 Write the addition sentence. Circle and cross out the ones leaving. Write the related subtraction sentence.

Use with Teacher's Edition pages 272A–272D.

Name ______________________

Problem Solving: Choose the Operation

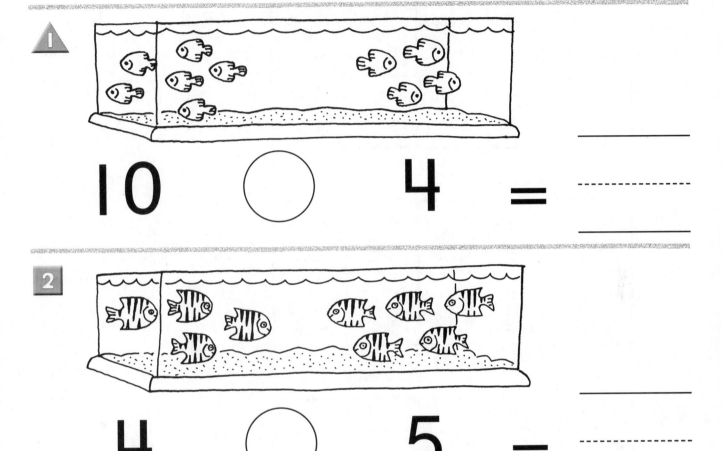

1

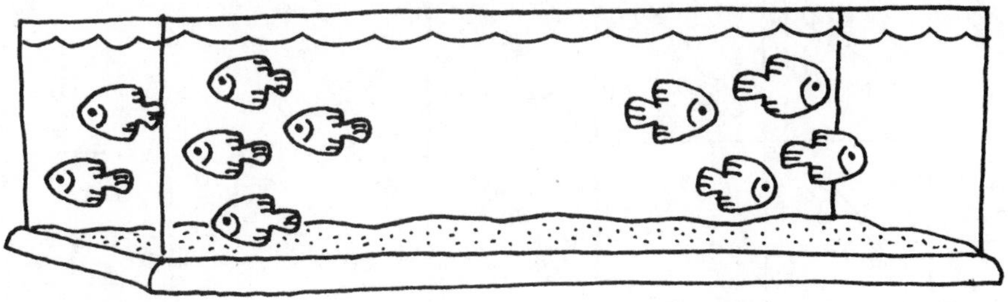

10 ○ 4 = ____

2

4 ○ 5 = ____

3

8 ○ 3 = ____

Directions: 1–3 Tell a story to match the picture. Decide if it shows addition or subtraction. Write a plus or minus sign in the circle. Write the answer.

Use with Teacher's Edition pages 273A–274.

Name ____________________

Practice 15.1

Numbers 10–12

1

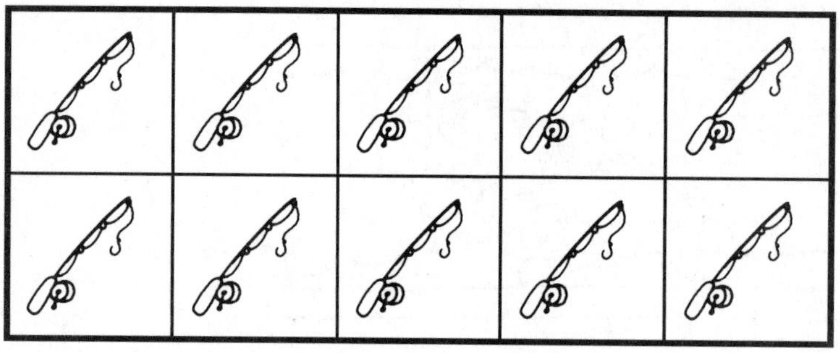

2

3

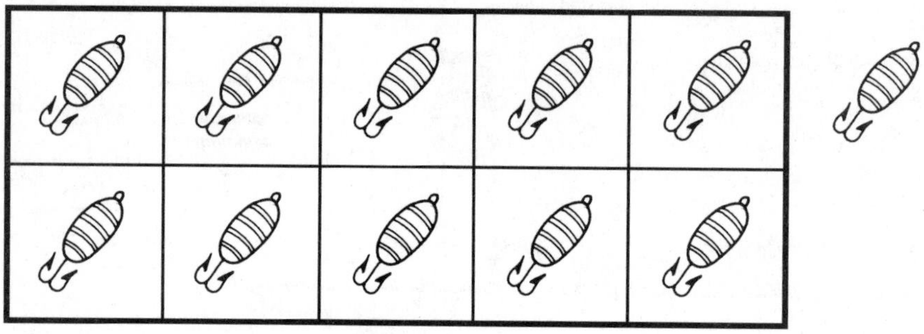

4

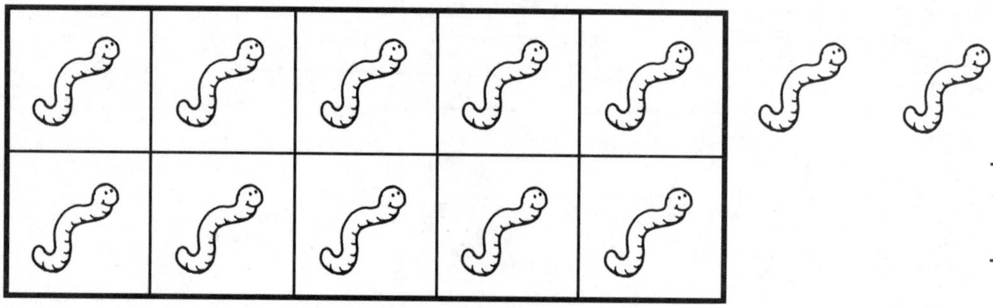

Directions: 1–4 Count the filled ten-frame as 10 and count on. Write the number.

Use with Teacher's Edition pages 285A–286.

Name ______________________

Practice 15.2

Numbers 13–14

1

2

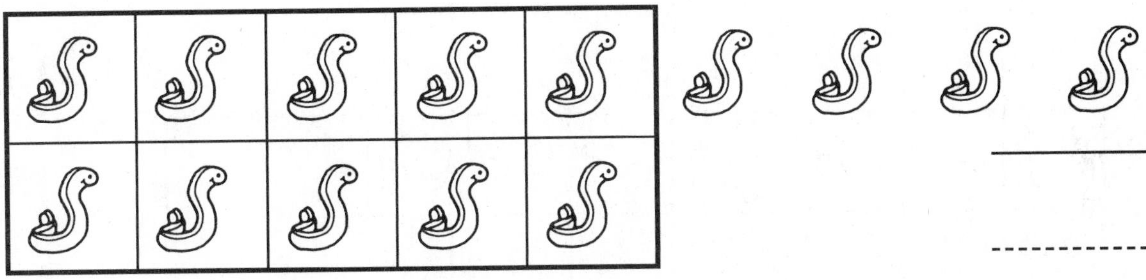

3

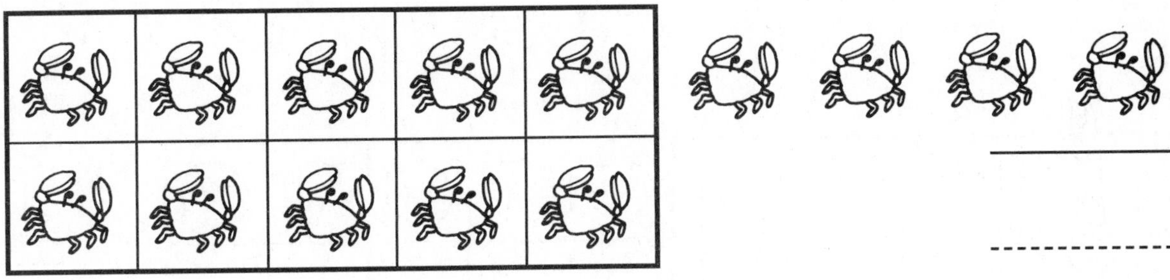

4

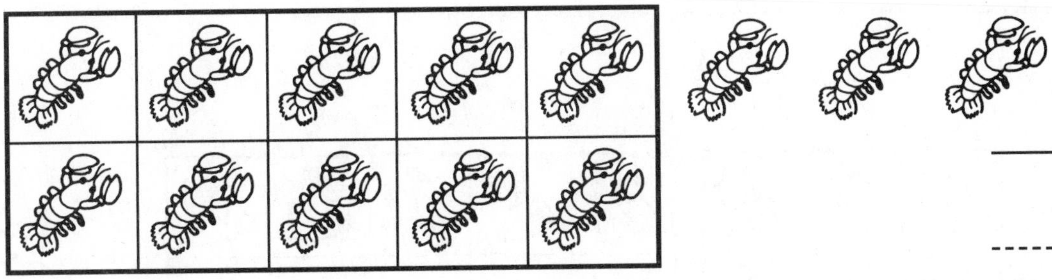

Directions: 1–4 Count the filled ten-frame as 10 and count on. Write the number.

Use with Teacher's Edition pages 287A–288.

Name ______________________

Practice 15.3

Numbers 15–16

1

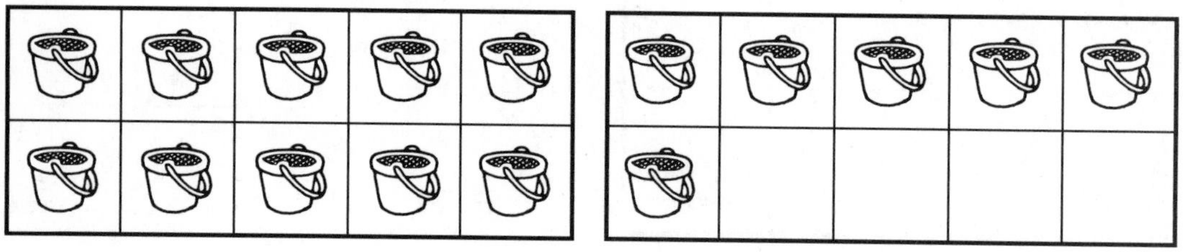

14

15

16

2

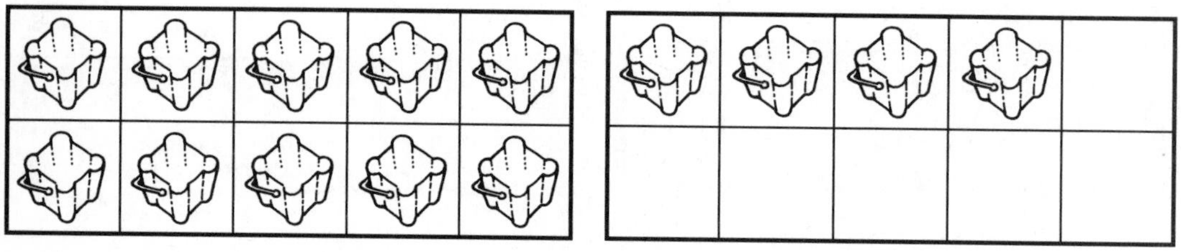

14

15

16

3

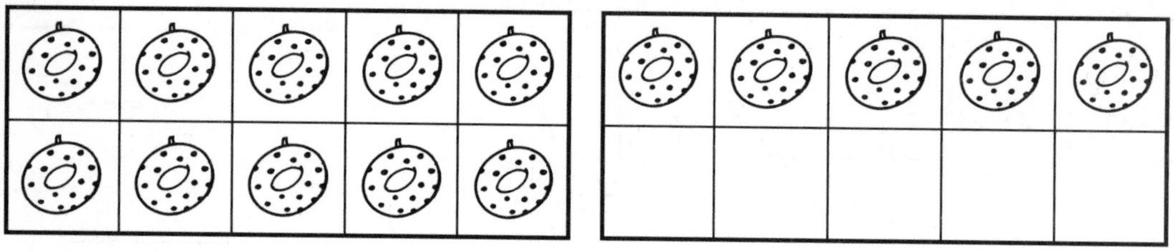

14

15

16

4

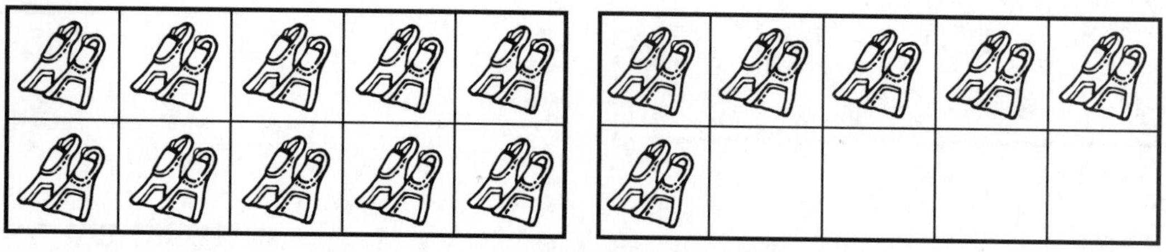

14

15

16

Directions: 1–4 Count the items. Circle the number.

Use with Teacher's Edition pages 289A–290.

Name ______________________

Practice 15.4

Numbers 17–18

1

17

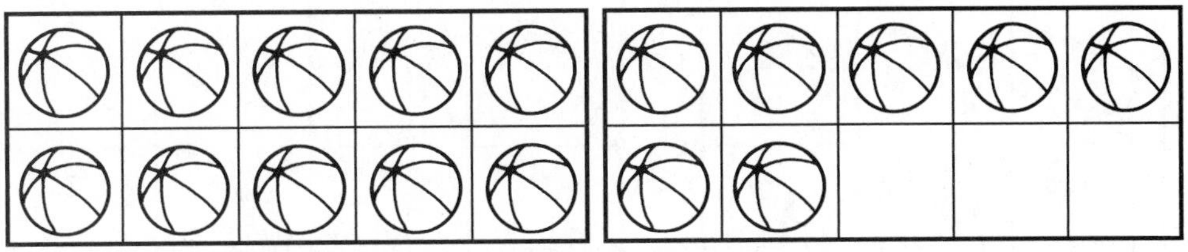

2

18

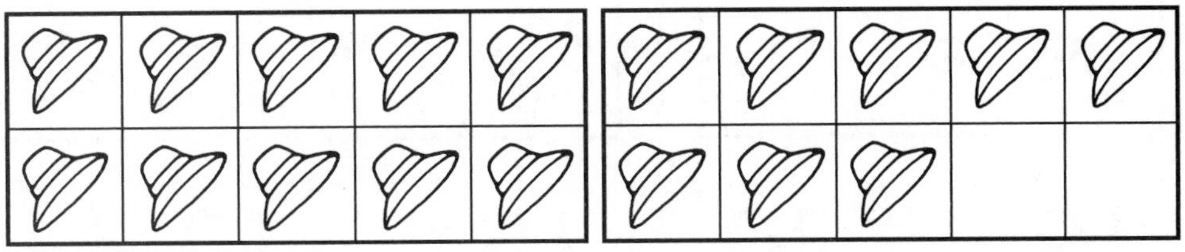

3

18

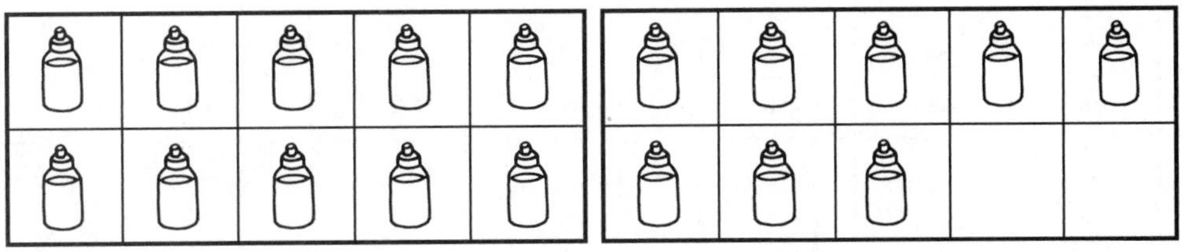

4

17

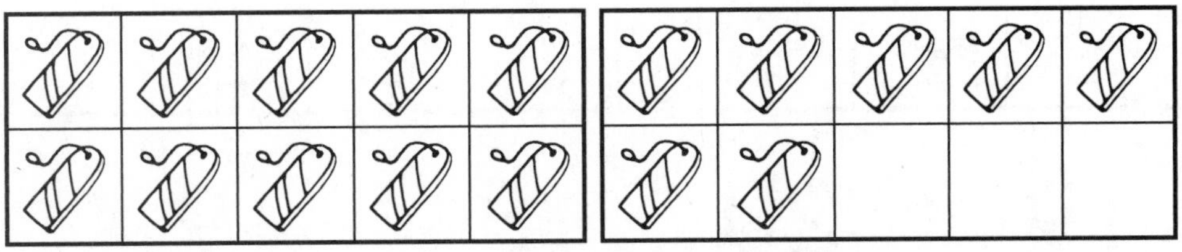

Directions: 1–4 Count the filled ten-frame as ten and count on. Write the number.

Use with Teacher's Edition pages 291A–292.

Name ______________________________

Numbers 19–20

1

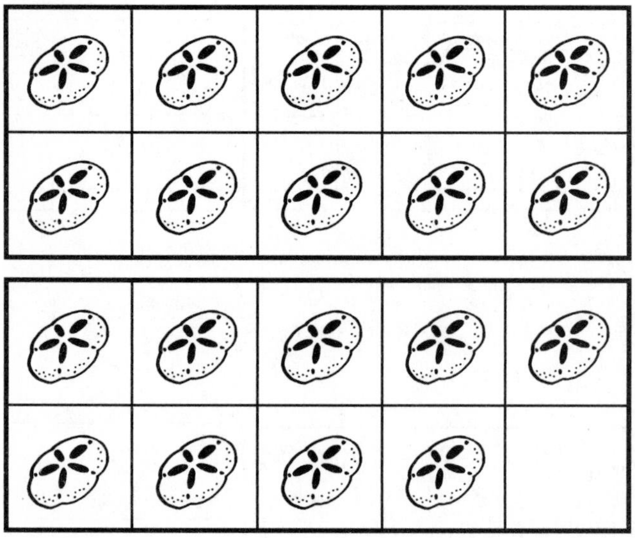

18 19 20

2

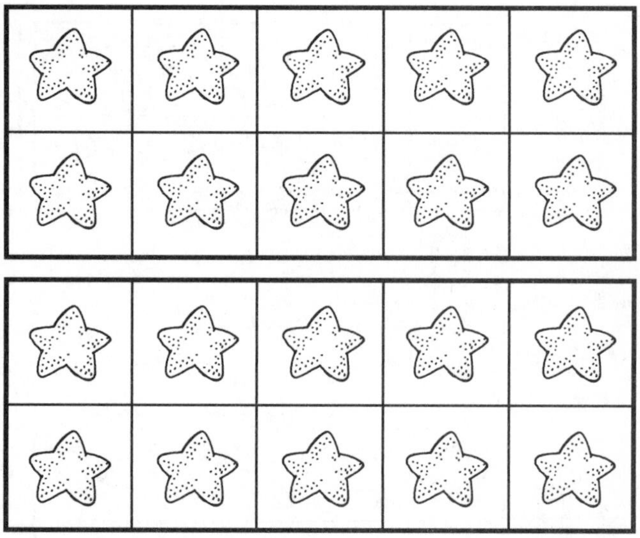

18 19 20

3

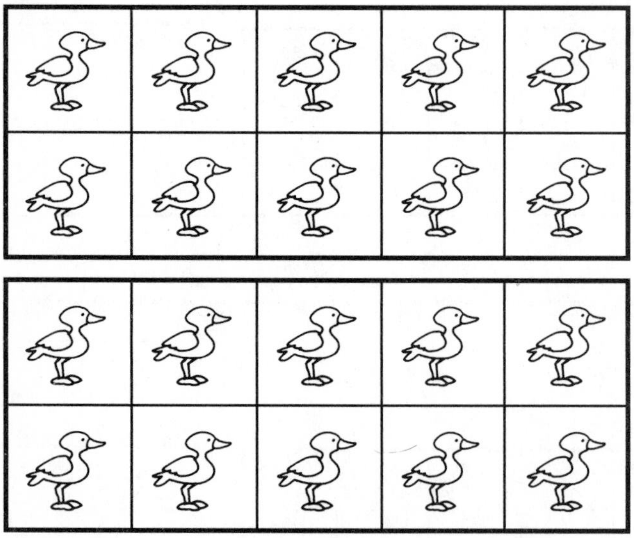

18 19 20

4

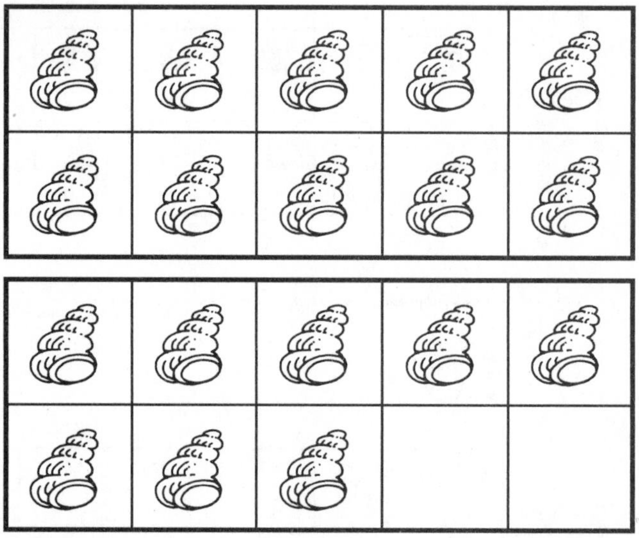

18 19 20

Directions: 1–4 Count the items. Circle the number.

Use with Teacher's Edition pages 293A–294.

Name ______________________

Practice 15.6

Order Numbers 10–20

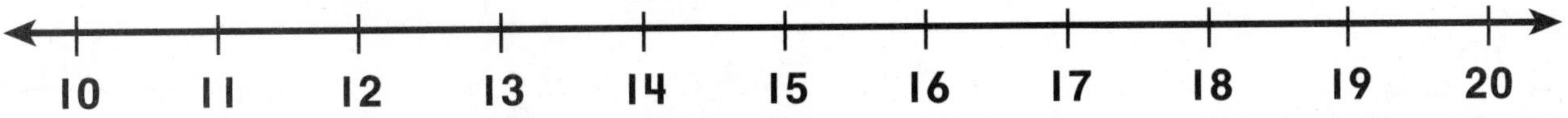

1

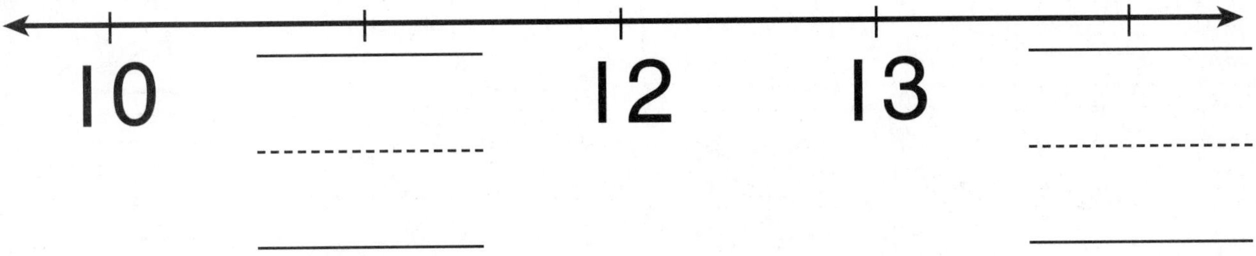

2

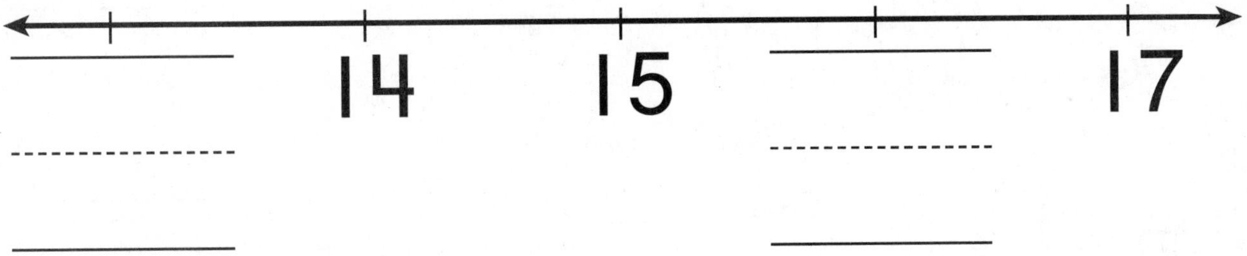

3

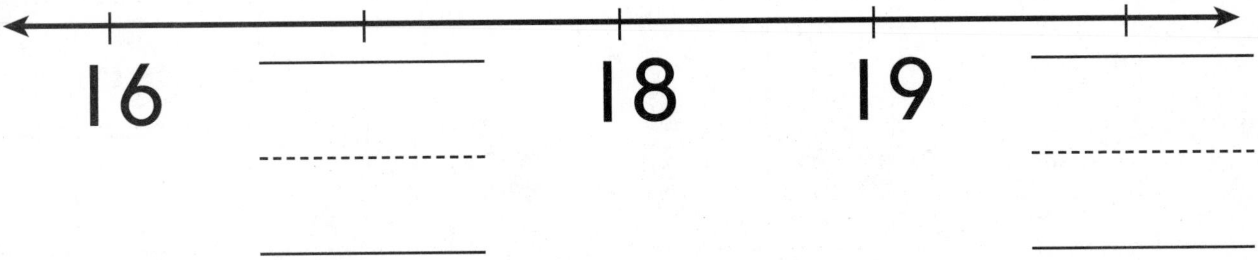

Directions: 1–3 Write the missing numbers.

Use with Teacher's Edition pages 295A–296.

Name ______________________

Dimes and Pennies

1 

________ ¢

2 

________ ¢

3 

________ ¢

4 

________ ¢

5 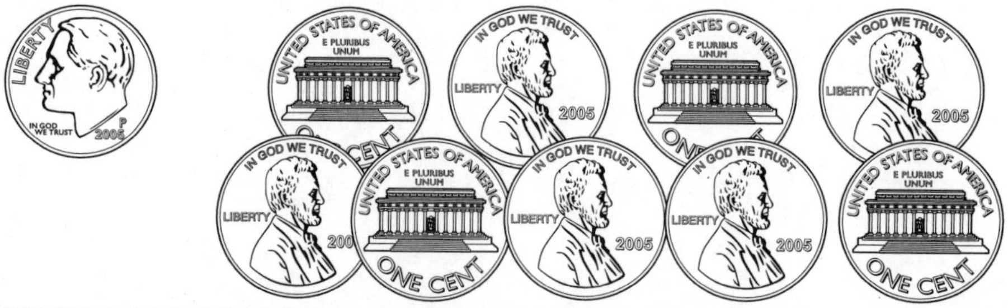

________ ¢

Directions: 1–5 Point to the dime and say "ten cents." Point to each penny as you count on the cents in all. Write the number of cents.

Use with Teacher's Edition pages 297A–298.

Name ______________________________

Practice 15.8

Estimating

1

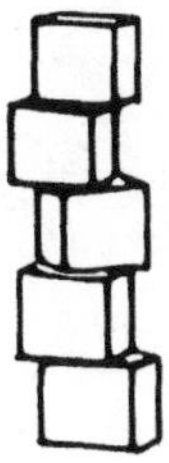

10

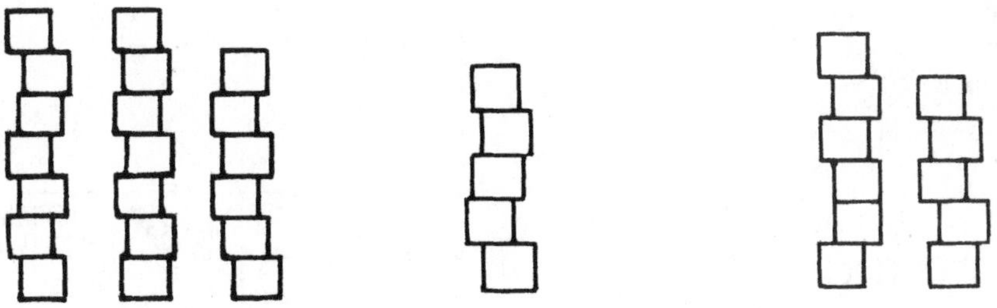

2

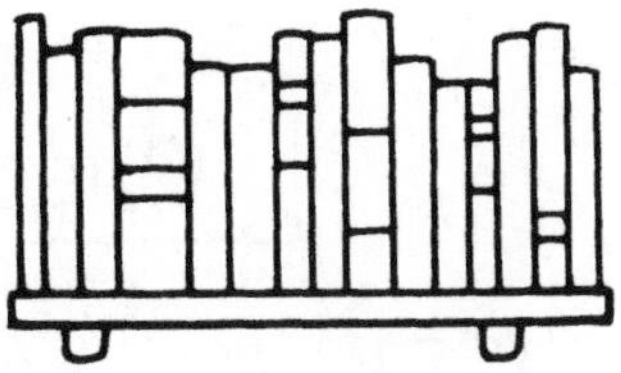

15

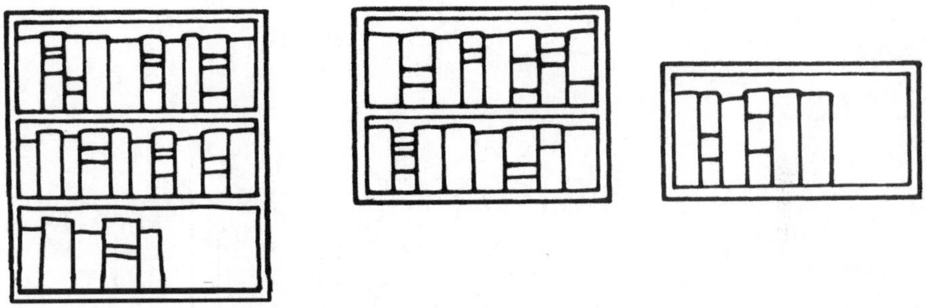

3

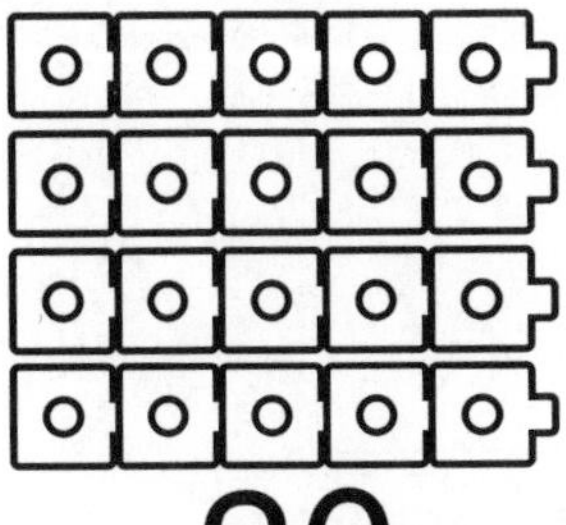

20

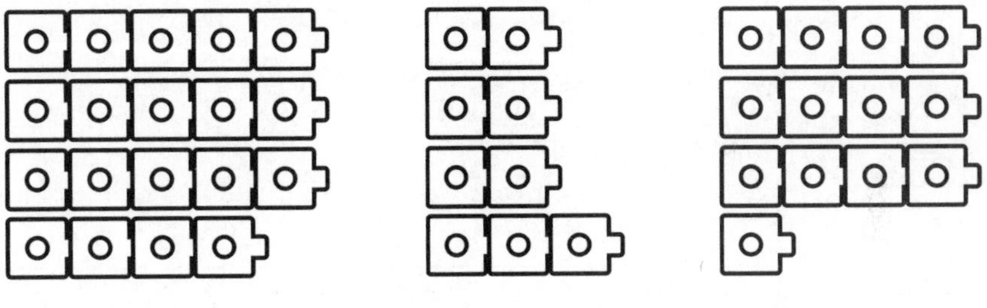

4

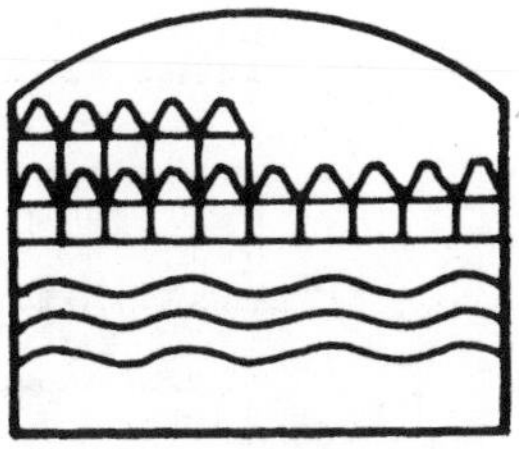

15

Directions: 1–4 Circle the set that has about the same number as the first set.

Use with Teacher's Edition pages 298A–298D.

Name ______________________

Problem Solving: Guess and Check

1

Guess

Check

more than 15

less than 15

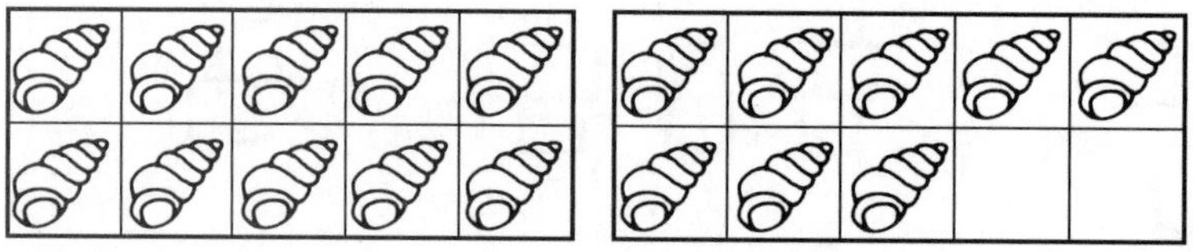

2

Guess

Check

more than 15

less than 15

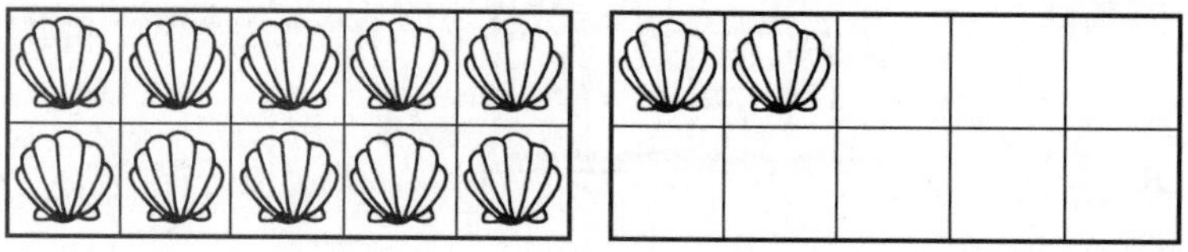

3

Guess

Check

more than 15

less than 15

4

Guess

Check

more than 15

less than 15

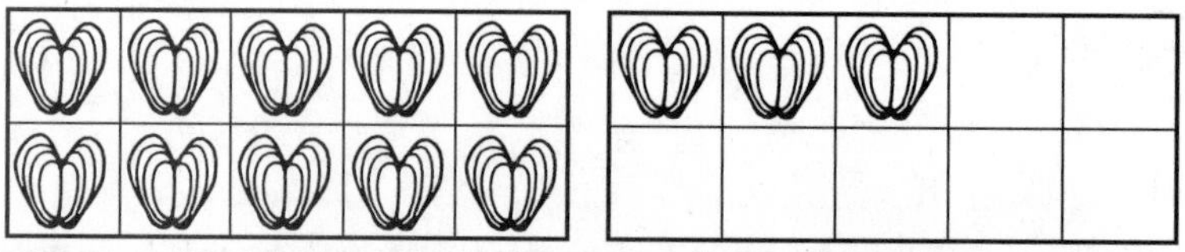

Directions: 1–4 Guess whether the picture shows more than 15 or less than 15. Circle your guess. Count to check your answer. Write the number.

Use with Teacher's Edition pages 299A–300.

Name ______________________

Practice 16.1

Numbers 21–25

1

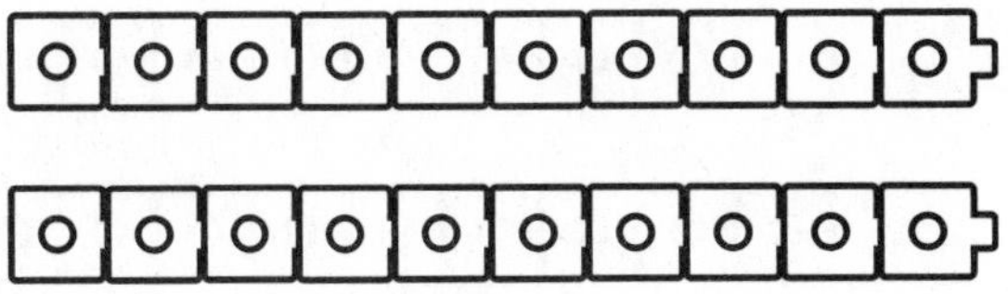

2

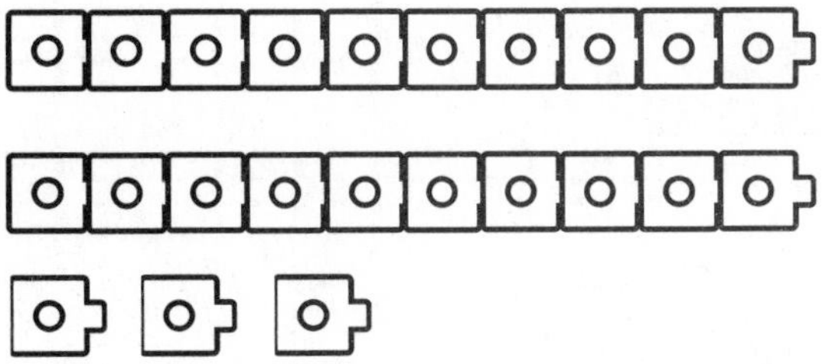

3

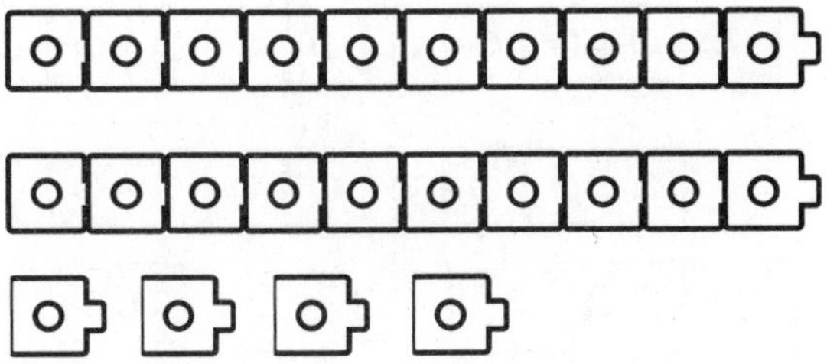

4

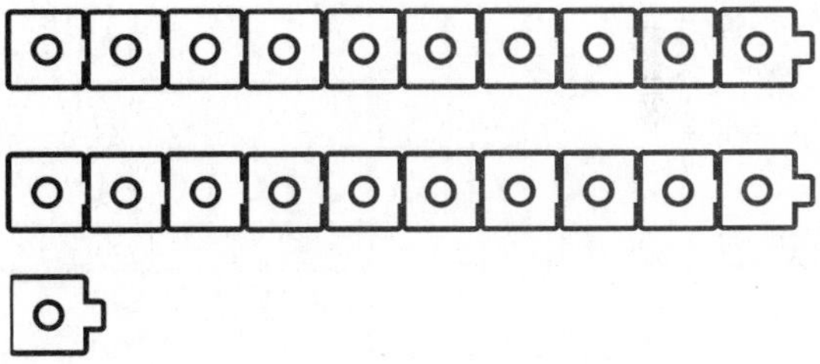

5

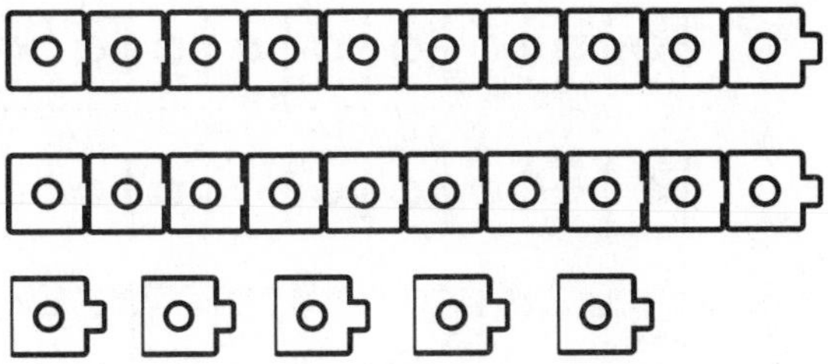

6

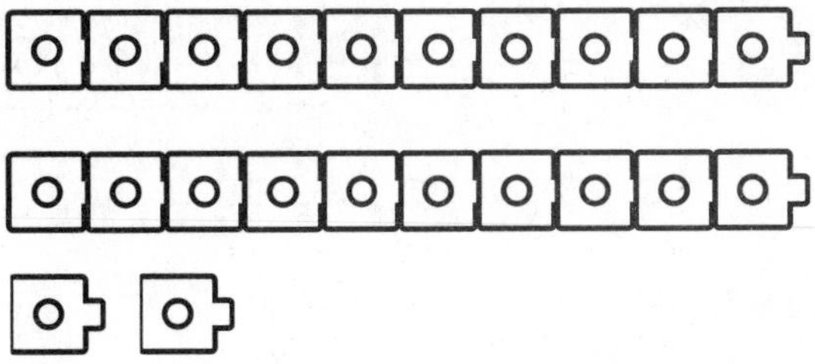

Directions: 1–6 Count the cube trains by tens and then count on. Write the number.

Use with Teacher's Edition pages 305A–306.

Name ______________________

Practice 16.2

Numbers 26–30

1
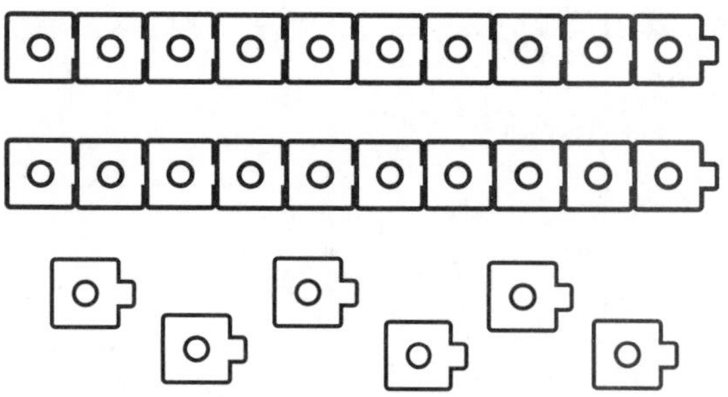

25 26 27

2
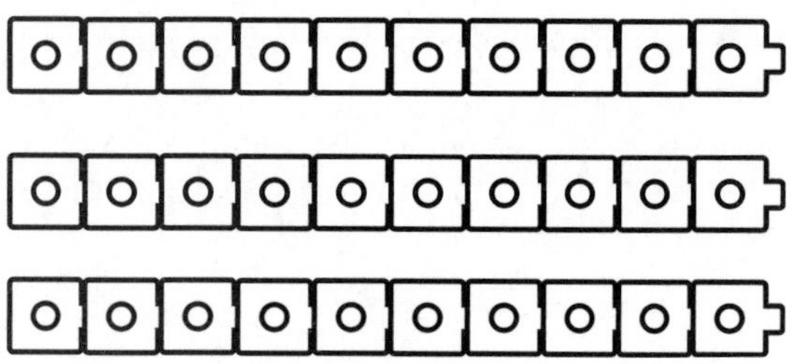

28 29 30

3
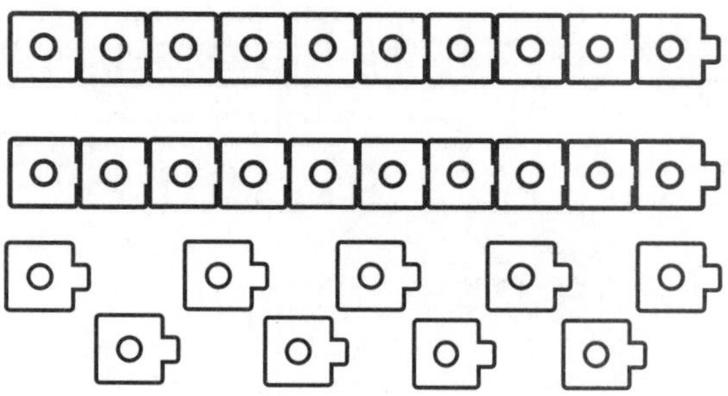

27 28 29

4
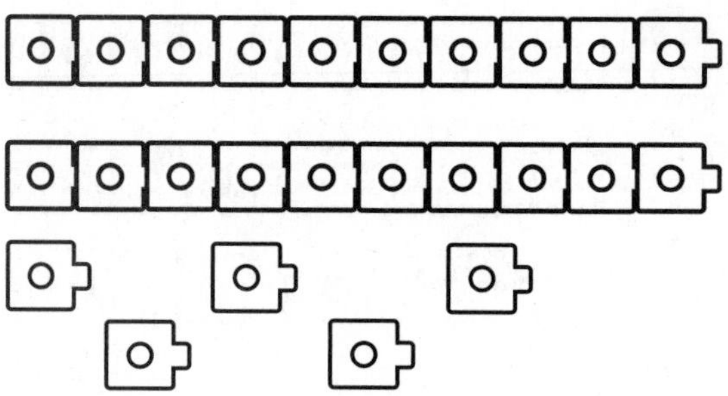

25 26 27

5
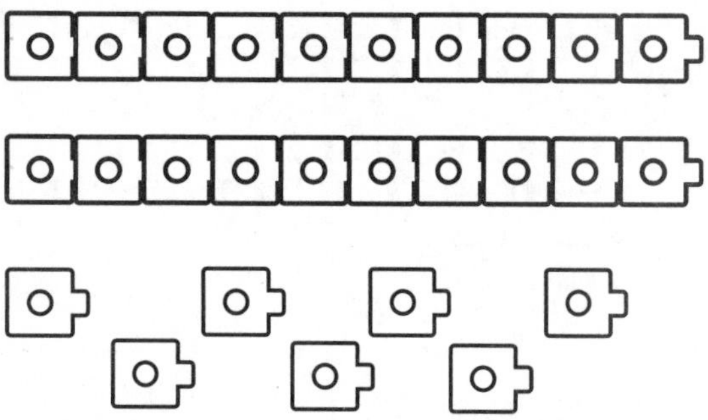

27 28 29

6
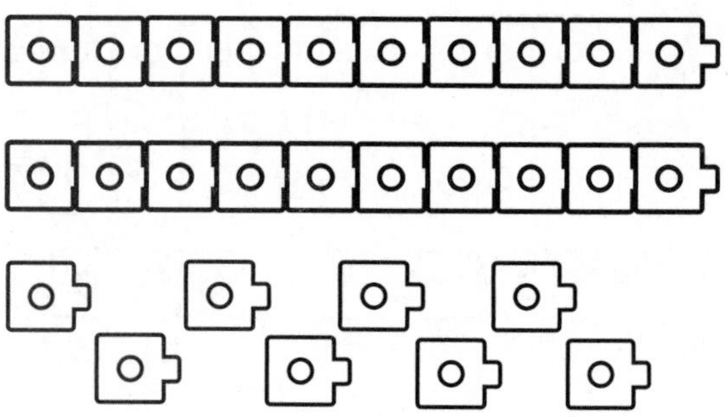

27 28 29

Directions: 1–6 Count the cube trains by tens and then count on. Circle the number.

Use with Teacher's Edition pages 307A–308.

Name ______________________

Practice 16.3

Order Numbers 1–31

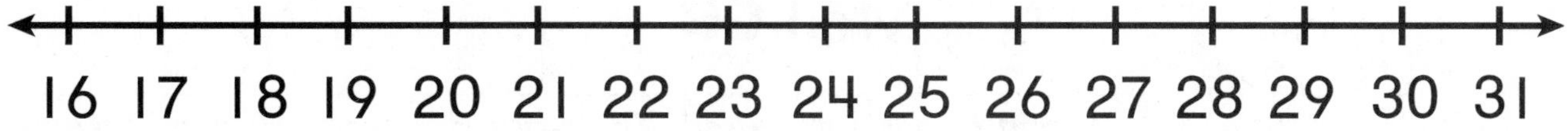

1. ____ 17 ____ 19

2. 20 ____ 22 ____

3. ____ 25 ____ 27

4. 28 ____ 30 ____

Directions: **1–5** Write the missing numbers.

Use with Teacher's Edition pages 308A–308D.

Name ____________________

Practice 16.4

Calendar: Using Numbers 1–31

March						
Sunday	Monday	Tuesday	Wednesday	Thursday	Friday	Saturday
	1	2		4	5	
7	8		10	11		13
14		16	17		19	20
	22		24	25		27
28		30				

Directions: Write the missing dates. Then circle each Tuesday. Put an X on the tenth, twentieth, and thirtieth days. Underline the day between the twenty first and the twenty third.

Use with Teacher's Edition pages 309A–310.

Name ____________________

Count by Twos, Fives, Tens

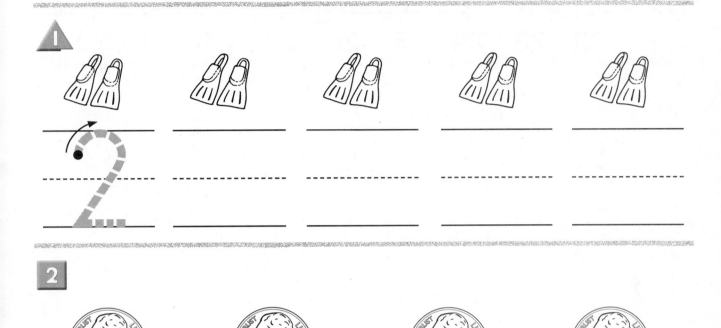

1

2 ______ ______ ______ ______

2

5 ¢ ______ ¢ ______ ¢ ______ ¢

3

10 ______ ______

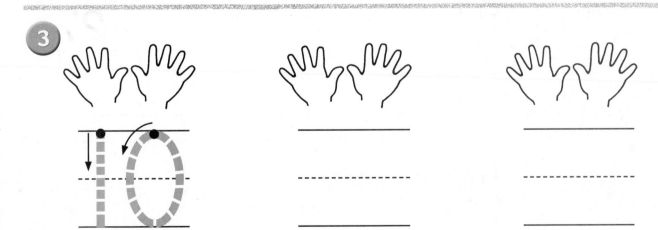

Directions: **1** Count by twos. Write the numbers. **2** Count by fives. Write the number of cents. **3** Count by tens. Write the numbers.

Use with Teacher's Edition pages 311A–312.

Name ______________________________

Practice 16.6

Problem Solving: Use a Pattern

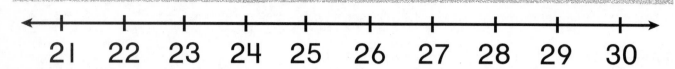

21	22	23	24	25	26	27	28	29	30

1. 22 ______ 24 ______ 26

2. 30 29 ______ ______ 26

3. 22 24 ______ 28 ______

4. 30 28 26 ______ ______

Directions: 1–4 Look for a pattern. Write the missing numbers. Use the number line to help.

Use with Teacher's Edition pages 313A–314.